Sow

How

A modern guide to grow-your-own veg

PAUL MATSON

LUCY ANNA SCOTT

PAVILION

Contents

Problem solving

Get growing!

Having at long last secured an allotment in Bristol, I paid a visit to my local garden centre. After several minutes of staring at wall-to-wall racks of seed packets, I started to feel out of my depth. Where to begin?

It was this experience that prompted me to design a small range of veg seed packets that would stand out from the crowd and appeal to anyone who, like me, was looking for a simple 'way in' to veg gardening.

A colourful, bold, graphic approach combined with clear growing advice, and SowHow was born. That then led to this book – a uniquely graphic guide to gardening that aims to show everything you need to know to get started.

The SowHow philosophy is simple: anyone, with the right support and encouragement, can grow their own tasty veg. But why bother? Firstly, it's about flavour. Fresh food – whether peas from the pod or sun-warmed tomatoes – tastes better. We pay a premium for seasonal, locally sourced organic produce from farmers' markets or veg box schemes, but you can grow similar crops at home – and you can't get more local than that.

We all know that vegetables are good for us and we're ever more conscious of what goes into our food and its environmental impact. Growing your own gives you control over how your food is raised. What's more, being outdoors and connecting with the soil is a welcome break from our screen-dominated lives. Digging and weeding is also a lot cheaper than going to the gym!

In this book you'll find easily available, traditional varieties alongside some more unusual suggestions. Yet another advantage of grow-your-own is the sheer diversity of seeds, many of which can be sourced online. You can also keep an eye out in early spring for seed swap events near you. These are a great way to meet other gardeners, who can pass on their local know-how.

If your garden is tiny or you're renting, or you only have a windowsill or balcony, there are still many things you can grow. Most of the veg in this book will happily grow in containers – there's plenty of advice for plants in pots.

Sadly, many people believe that they weren't born with green fingers. Part of the problem is that the gardening industry continues to insist that gardening is really easy. When reality doesn't match expectation, we blame ourselves.

The truth is that, while growing most veg isn't effortless, it does get easier with practice. The 'Things to know' section gives pointers to success, but do take heart that even the most experienced gardeners lose plants. Many, in fact, play a numbers game – growing much more than they actually need in the likelihood that some seeds won't germinate, some seedlings will be nibbled by pests and some plants just won't flower or fruit.

In our fast-paced lives we often demand instant results. Plants require – in fact *teach* – patience. Give your plot time and love, and it will reward you. There's something magical about helping a tiny seed become a plant that feeds you. I hope you find encouragement and inspiration in this book to grow, sow, look after and eat a bountiful and delicious harvest that you can enjoy with friends and family.

Paul Matson

First things first

Once you've decided to grow your own veg, it can be tempting to hurry to the garden centre, stack the trolley with as many plants as your car can hold, and set about creating your garden on a wing and a prayer. But knowing some basics about your site will pay dividends at harvest time.

Wind

Wind dries and erodes soil. It also stresses stems and foliage. A breezy garden need not stunt your ambitions but as you plan your garden, think about protection for your plants. Do avoid solid barriers, such as fences, which intensify the strength of the wind on plants. Instead, opt for semi-permeable materials, such as hedges or willow hurdles.

Frost

The topography of a garden influences its microclimate. If you're situated on a slope, you may find that cold air rolls to the lowest point, collecting in depressions against fences, walls and hedges. These areas are known as 'frost pockets'. If your garden is affected, you will notice a morning mist that lingers in your garden. Avoid planting tender species in frost pockets.

Sun

Plants need light to make food and some need more light than others. So, some basic facts to establish are: whether your garden is south or north-facing, how much light and warmth it gets daily and where the sunlight falls and when. SunEarthTools.com is an online tool that allows you to see the course of the sun during the day at your exact location. Plan to position your containers, raised beds and borders in the sunniest, brightest spot you have available; most veg need six to eight hours of direct sunlight a day. If your garden is very shady, grow leafy veg, such as spinach and lettuce, as they tolerate these conditions.

Soil

Healthy soil is crucial, so understanding your soil's condition allows you to fix issues in time for the growing season. Grab a handful of your soil and do a squeeze test (see p.22) to reveal how well drained it is and how quickly it warms up. Then dig up a large clod to see if it's busy with worms. If it is, you'll also have the beneficial microbes and bacteria necessary for fertile soil (see p.38). Also, pick up a soil-testing kit from the garden centre, which will tell you your soil's pH. This is worth knowing since highly acid or highly alkaline soils can upset plants (see p.22). If you have very poor soil quality, make your garden in containers or raised beds filled with fresh compost.

Budget

It's tempting to spend lots of cash on plants in the beginning and overwhelm yourself with care responsibilities. But designing your garden to suit the money and time you have to spare will lead to a more rewarding experience. For the first year, try out a handful of easy-to-grow veg like beetroot, rocket or mizuna, perhaps with a couple of quirky veg added to the mix. Keeping things simple will build your confidence. It's also fun – and highly achievable – to make a productive garden on a tiny budget. Seed swaps, for instance, are a fantastic way to pick up seeds cheaply.

Young and old

Plan your plot to make it engaging for any kids, friends and family you'd like to involve. Incorporate brightly coloured, aromatic plants for kids to explore. And quick-growing crops, like radish or microherbs, will sustain their enthusiasm. Could you afford to put a small growing space aside for them? For those with restricted mobility, beds raised to waist level will make digging, sowing and watering easier. And long-handled tools enable you to dig while sitting down.

Make a garden anywhere

Large gardens or allotments are not easy to come by but luckily you can assemble a flourishing veg plot on almost any scrap of ground – in fact, you can do it without any ground space at all. Here are a few ideas.

Upside-down planters
Plants needn't take valuable floor space; you can create a growing space out of thin air. Buy upside-down planters or make them from large tin cans, PET bottles or even plastic buckets. These make fantastic homes for herbs, tomatoes (indeterminate varieties, see p.87), cucumbers and peppers – well out of the way of pests and weeds.

Raised beds
You can create raised beds on hard surfaces and almost any vegetable will thrive in them. Build your own with reclaimed wood and line them with polythene. Ensure they're at least 45cm (18in) deep so that plants have enough space to root. One advantage of a raised bed is that you can start with weed-free soil. Beds can also be set waist-high for 'no-bend' gardening.

Wheelbarrows
Wheelbarrows with holes drilled in the bottom make ideal portable gardens that can be parked on a patio or pavement. If you have room to spare, you can place containers around them, too. Wheel the barrow around to catch the sun or put it under shelter if heavy rain is forecast.

Upended wooden pallets

This eye-catching vertical solution (see pp.12–13) needs nothing more than an outdoor wall, fence or railing to lean against. Just make sure you choose a sunny spot. They make ideal gardens for herbs and strawberries or try alternating rows of herbs with rows of flowers for extra pzazz.

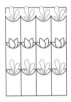

Shoe organizers

These organizers are perfect for modular gardening. Use canvas organizers and fill the individual pockets with soil, up to 4cm (1½in) below the lip. Experiment with herbs and lettuce mixes. A couple of tips: plant any moisture-loving plants in the lower pockets and, since water can discolour the canvas, it is a good idea to opt for darker fabric.

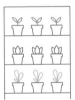

Recycled shelving units

Enlist a redundant shelving unit as a vertical planting solution. Each shelf can house pots with a different crop – try herbs, salad leaves, radish and microgreens. Place next to a sunny window and rotate the pots regularly so they catch the light on all sides.

Plastic tubs

An old plastic tub with holes punched in the bottom can be kept in the sunniest spot you can spare or just by the doorstep. Check out our 'good companion' suggestions for ideas of plants to grow together (see pp.50–173).

⊕ Know how – Build a pallet garden

You'll need:

1 good-quality pallet (with no splits in the wood)

Landscape fabric

Staple gun and 5mm (¼in) staples

Scissors

Compost

Lay the pallet on its front. Fold the landscape fabric double and use to cover the back of the pallet – a bit like a sheet snugly covering the top and sides of a bed. Staple at frequent intervals along three sides of the pallet, leaving one side open. Then staple the fabric to the back of the pallet – anywhere the fabric meets the wood. The fabric needs to be snug to the wood so it's strong enough to hold soil.

Trim the excess fabric.

Stand the pallet on its end, with the unstapled fabric at the top. Fill with compost through the unstapled side.

Plant seedlings into the soil. To allow for root growth, arrange the seedlings in an offset fashion.

Water daily until plants are established, and regularly thereafter. Give an organic feed once a month. Stand the pallet upright and lean against a wall or fence.

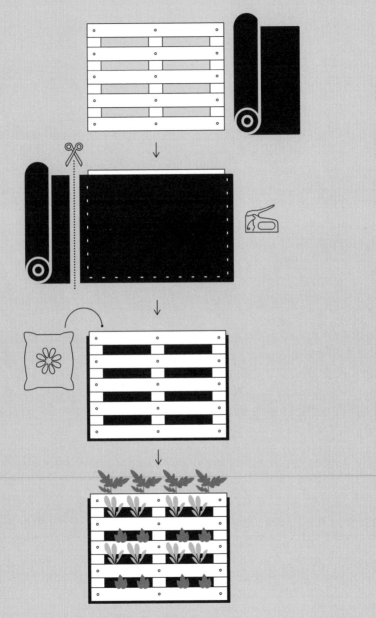

Container talk

Plants will thrive in any container, provided it has drainage holes and plenty of space for roots to breathe and grow. Your crops may need to be transplanted into one or two successively larger pots before they are ready to go in their final positions outside or they may spend their entire lives in the same container.

Basic container needs

SEED TRAYS
Short-term homes for seedlings

7.5CM (3IN) POTS
For potting on sturdy seedlings, giving them more room to grow

9CM (3½IN) POTS
For larger, 7.5cm (3in), plug plants that need a little more time indoors

Recycled planters
There's a world of DIY pot options; just add holes in the bottom where needed.

 Milk cartons: Cut in half and use the bottom for small plants and the upper half as cloches

 Egg cartons: Excellent for starting off seedlings

 Newspaper: Use to cover the sides and one end of a toilet roll tube to make a biodegradable pot

 Fruit punnets: Ready-made seed trays

 Tin cans: Just add holes in the bottom

 Plastic storage boxes: Use to plant up a salad or herb garden

The pros and cons of traditional containers

Clay
PROS: Porous to air and water. Thick walls retain heat, which protects roots. Sturdy, so will not blow over easily, but breakable if dropped. Good for plants that like dry soil, such as cacti. **CONS:** Can dry out quickly in full sun.

Plastic
PROS: Excellent for moisture-loving plants. Requires less watering than clay. Lightweight for balconies and easily moved. **CONS:** Thin walls, so roots aren't very well insulated. High environmental impact.

Natural and recycled stone
PROS: Long-lasting. Good heat insulation.
CONS: Heavy, hard to move around.

Growbags
PROS: Great portable gardens. Hold large volumes of soil. Cheap. **CONS:** Tricky to water plants properly.

Upside-down planters
PROS: Fantastic for small spaces. Good pest prevention – no slugs! Excellent aeration. No weeds. Ideal for a 'no-bend' garden. **CONS:** Dry out quickly in sun.

Hanging baskets
PROS: No floor space needed. Available in sustainable materials such as coir. Great for herbs, tomatoes and alpine strawberries. **CONS:** Messy when watering.

Things
to know

Once you have decided where to pitch your plot, the next step is to consider how to create a nurturing environment. Working with the soil, the light and the whims of the sky is part and parcel of cultivating healthy, happy plants. And here, we show you how.

Light and shade

Plants rely on sunlight to provide the energy they need for growth. Leaves, which function like solar panels, are expert at enabling the process of photosynthesis to take place. But there are ways that gardeners can help, too.

RIGHT PLANT, RIGHT PLACE: South-facing gardens are ideal as they capture more daylight. But if buildings or trees heavily shade your garden, planting in hanging baskets or on rooftops that are out of the shade, could be an alternative.

LIGHT AND MIRRORS: Paint walls and fences white or in a light shade, or use mirrors to reflect light back onto plants. You could line shelves of a mini greenhouse with foil. Make sure you keep windows of greenhouses clean so they let in as much sunlight as possible.

SIGNS AND SYMPTOMS: If your plant is light-deprived, seedlings' stems will grow very spindly as they stretch to find the sun. While light is very important for plants, they shouldn't get too hot – you may need to shade your crops if they show signs of wilting, or move them to a cooler spot.

LIGHT BOOST: Grow lamps can be used where there is no naturally occurring light or in other situations. They can be useful for indoor-grown plants. Seeds need cool white fluorescent lamps, which provide blue light. Flowering plants need broad-spectrum fluorescent lamps to promote fruit and flower production.

How much sun is enough?

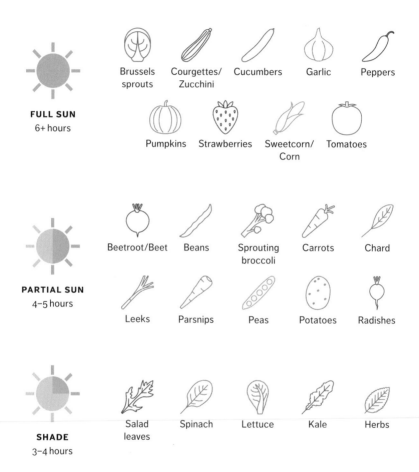

FULL SUN
6+ hours

Brussels sprouts · Courgettes/Zucchini · Cucumbers · Garlic · Peppers · Pumpkins · Strawberries · Sweetcorn/Corn · Tomatoes

PARTIAL SUN
4–5 hours

Beetroot/Beet · Beans · Sprouting broccoli · Carrots · Chard · Leeks · Parsnips · Peas · Potatoes · Radishes

SHADE
3–4 hours

Salad leaves · Spinach · Lettuce · Kale · Herbs

A handy rule to keep in mind is that leafy vegetables tolerate low light levels (partial shade), root veg and legumes are fine in medium levels (half a day of sunshine) and fruit requires the most light (full sun).

Working with weather

It's little wonder that gardeners get obsessed with weather forecasts. Plants need sun, rain and wind, but extremes can cause irreversible crop damage. While there's nothing you can do to change the weather, you can protect your plants.

STRONG SUN: Leaves may wilt on a hot summer's day because they are losing water quicker than they can drink it up from the soil. Shading plants – especially seedlings – from too much direct sun can help.

HEAVY RAIN: Waterlogged soils contain very little of the oxygen that's vital for plant roots. Improve soggy soils by digging your plot in autumn. You can improve drainage by adding horticultural sand.

DROUGHT: When all available water in the soil has gone, plants can wilt and die. Ensure this does not happen by checking moisture levels regularly, particularly on very hot days.

HIGH WIND: Strong winds can snap climbers, erode soil and dry out leaves. Solid barriers, like brick walls, result in strong turbulence on the other side. Air-permeable fences and screens are better.

FROST: Some plants are able to cope with frost but many are sensitive to cold weather. These are known as 'frost-tender' plants and should not be planted outside until all danger of spring frost has passed, usually around early summer.

Frost tolerance

How cold can they go? Some crops need care and attention in chilly weather, while others are self-sufficient.

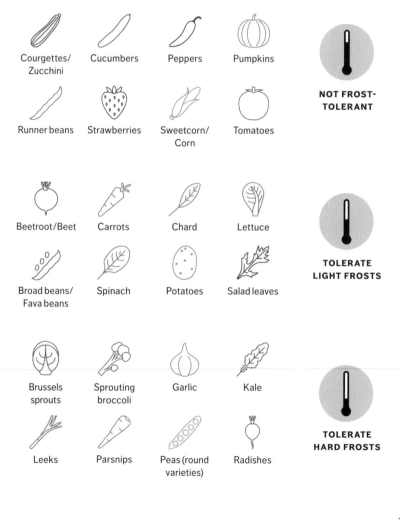

Courgettes/ Zucchini   Cucumbers   Peppers   Pumpkins

Runner beans   Strawberries   Sweetcorn/ Corn   Tomatoes

NOT FROST-TOLERANT

Beetroot/Beet   Carrots   Chard   Lettuce

Broad beans/ Fava beans   Spinach   Potatoes   Salad leaves

TOLERATE LIGHT FROSTS

Brussels sprouts   Sprouting broccoli   Garlic   Kale

Leeks   Parsnips   Peas (round varieties)   Radishes

TOLERATE HARD FROSTS

Getting to know your soil

Healthy soil is the foundation of healthy plants. The condition of your soil influences the success – and flavour – of your veg gardening efforts. A good soil enables plants to source valuable nutrients, moisture and oxygen.

⊕ Know how – DIY soil test

Clay, sand and silt are common soil textures found in gardens. It is really useful for growers to understand which type of soil they are working with. Grab a handful of soil and give it a squeeze. If it falls apart easily, then you have a sandy soil. If it clumps together and you can roll it into a sausage, your soil is clay. A silt soil feels silky to the touch. Loam is somewhere in between; it is ideal for growing plants but is very rare.

Get an indication of how rich your soil is in organic matter by digging some up and watching for worms. If there are none, your soil is probably low in nutrients. Improve this by adding compost or manure over time (see pp.24–25).

In urban gardens, you may find that the soil contains bricks and rubble. If your soil is poor-quality like this, or contaminated, you may prefer to use raised beds filled with fresh soil (see p.10) – especially if you're growing food.

Why soil pH matters

Soil pH is a measure of soil's acidity or alkalinity. The organisms in soil can generally tolerate either an acid or alkaline soil, though the nutrients available to plants can vary depending on the soil's pH. A good range for plant growth is 5.5–7.5, with the optimum level being 6.5. When starting a new vegetable plot, it is worth checking your soil pH with a DIY soil-testing kit or pH meter.

pH levels

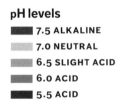

7.5 ALKALINE
7.0 NEUTRAL
6.5 SLIGHT ACID
6.0 ACID
5.5 ACID

Your garden soil texture is fixed, so you cannot change it by cultivation or by adding better soil to your garden. But understanding its strengths and weaknesses will help you work with it.

CLAY SOIL
Heavy to dig, high in nutrients;
cold in the winter, bakes and cracks
in the summer

SANDY SOIL
Light, dry and low
in nutrients; warms
easily in spring

LOAM
An equal mix of clay,
silt and sand; fertile and
well-drained; rare

SILT SOIL
Fertile and light but retains
moisture; prone to getting
a crust on the surface;
easily compacted

Choosing compost

There are many different composts available – from general-purpose compost to those that are more specialized. Use the best quality you can afford, ensure it is fresh, and try to make sustainable choices by using soil from renewable sources.

MULTI-PURPOSE COMPOST: Can be used at any stage of growth; is cheaper than specific-use composts

ERICACEOUS COMPOST: Lime-free for acid-loving plants. Azaleas, heathers, blueberries and camellias

SEED COMPOST: This is free-draining and can hold plenty of moisture. Both qualities are necessary for seeds to germinate. Contains low levels of fertilizer

POTTING COMPOST: Use this for young seedlings or rooted cuttings, but not seeds. Nutrient levels are right for encouraging further growth but would damage seeds

$\rightarrow$ Know how – John Innes explained

Well-known in horticulture, John Innes mixes are seed and potting compost recipes, designed to support plants through all stages of growth. JI seed compost is for sowing seed. JI No 1 is for pricking out or potting up young seedlings or rooted cuttings. JI No 2 is for general potting of most houseplants and vegetable plants into medium-sized pots. JI No 3 is for final re-potting of hungry vegetable plants and for mature foliage plants and shrubs.

What's in multi-purpose compost?

Multi-purpose compost, the bags of soil that you buy from garden centres, is made from a mixture of loam, peat (or ideally a peat alternative; see below), sand and fertilizer. It is commonly referred to as 'compost' but true compost is actually the product of your compost bin (see pp.26–27).

Renewable peat alternatives

Peat provides excellent water-holding capacity, aeration and structure. But it is a non-renewable material, harvested from bogs that formed very, very slowly, years ago. Once peat bogs vanish, co-dependent plants and animals are lost and cannot be replaced. These peat-free composts offer more sustainable alternatives:

 Composted bark: Provides excellent aeration and drainage

 Leaf mould: Homemade mixes of leaves, rich in micro-organisms

 Coir: Coconut fibre – airy and water-retentive

 Garden compost: Straight from the compost bin, nutrient-rich

 Mushroom compost: Left over from mushroom farming, a great soil conditioner

 Worm compost: Ideal in mixes needing plenty of nutrients, with great water-holding capacity

Animal manures as soil conditioners

Well-rotted manure can be dug into soils, improving plant growth and yield.

FARMYARD MANURE
Attracts worms to the soil and increases soil fertility

CHICKEN MANURE
Sold as pellets; a great source of nitrogen

ZOO POO
'Exotic manure' with sky-high nitrogen levels

Making compost

Garden compost is a mix of rotted-down kitchen waste and other wet 'green' material, plus dry 'brown' material. Good compost contains the right amount of water, oxygen and worms. Here's what should be in your bin and what should not.

Greens: for adding nitrogen

 Fruit and vegetables: Peelings and other scraps

 Eggshells: Broken and crushed

 Coffee grounds: May also help repel slugs and snails

 Tea leaves and bags: Tip the leaves in but recycle the bag

 Cut flowers: Check that they're not diseased

 Grass clippings: Let them dry out before adding

Browns: for adding carbon

 Dry leaves: Brown, dead, fallen (but not diseased) leaves

 Straw: Slow to decompose; perfect for heavy soil

 Cardboard: Soaks up excess moisture

 Paper: Avoid glossy magazines

 Wool: Great water-retaining qualities

 Vacuum cleaner lint: Packed with organic material

Don't compost

 Meat and fish scraps: May attract pests

 Pet waste: Contains harmful bacteria

 Coal ash: Could be harmful to plants

 Bread: May attract pests

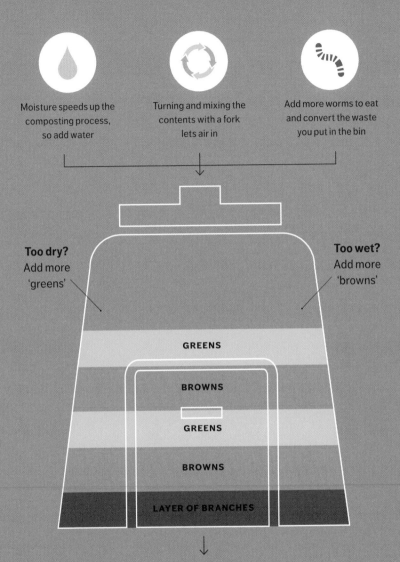

Moisture speeds up the composting process, so add water

Turning and mixing the contents with a fork lets air in

Add more worms to eat and convert the waste you put in the bin

Too dry?
Add more
'greens'

Too wet?
Add more
'browns'

GREENS

BROWNS

GREENS

BROWNS

LAYER OF BRANCHES

Start with a layer of twigs and branches, then build layers, alternating between green and brown material. Your compost is ready when you have a dark, rich soil layer at the bottom of the bin.

Mulch magic

Mulch is a layer of material added to the surface of the soil. It improves soil condition and thus creates a supportive environment for roots and plants.

Why and how to mulch

Healthy soil holds water well, is warm and weed-free, and hosts plenty of beneficial organisms. Organic mulch provides all of these. It is best applied in spring or autumn, when the soil is warm and moist; if the soil is too cold or dry, mulch won't be as effective. Water the soil so that it's moist and remove any weeds. Provide a 5cm (2in) thick layer but leave a mulch-free gap around the stems of plants. Wait until it has completely rotted down before adding more. For free mulch, try asking your local tree surgeon for shredded wood chips.

INSULATES: Mulches act as insulators, keeping the soil warmer during cool weather and cooler in warm months

RETAINS MOISTURE: A layer of mulch locks in soil moisture and also protects soil from heavy rainfall and erosion

PROTECTS ROOTS: Mulches improve the structure of the soil, which usually increases root growth

STOPS WEEDS: Mulch prevents light reaching any weeds trying to germinate beneath the surface

A choice of organic mulches

There is a world of organic mulches out there, just waiting for you. Our handy guide explains what they all are.

 Leaf mould: Make your own by gathering fallen leaves in autumn and letting them rot down

 Compost: A free source of mulch if you have a compost bin. Or you may be able to obtain bags of compost from your local council

 Well-rotted farmyard manure: Provides the soil with plant nutrients as it decomposes

 Mushroom compost: Try and source from a local mushroom farm

 Bark chippings: An aesthetically appealing mulch that improves soil as it rots

 Conifer bark: Decorative nuggets of pine and cypress trees

 Straw: Oat, wheat or soya bean straw for use on strawberries

 Dry seaweed: Slugs and snails are repelled by its sharp edges

 Grass clippings: Leave clippings on the lawn to dry out, then spread about your patch

A choice of decorative mulches

You can use non-biodegradable mulches – such as stones, pebbles or gravel. They are largely decorative but don't need replacing.

 Stones and pebbles: Low-maintenance; just keep them out of beds

 Shingle or gravel: Great for rock gardens

 Sea shells: Make an attractive white groundcover

 Landscape fabric: A porous layer for suppressing weeds

Buying seeds

Every seed contains an embryonic plant that's waiting for suitable conditions in which to germinate. Seeds want to grow, so raising them isn't as complicated as you might think.

Reading a seed packet
Seeds allow gardeners endless opportunities to explore a variety of flavours, shapes and colours.
- Check the sowing date: is it too late or too early?
- Check the 'use by' date. Fresh is best.
- Check the quantity. Is it more than you'll need?
- Do these seeds need to be started indoors?

Types of seed

OPEN-POLLINATED
Needs to be pollinated by insects, birds, wind or people. Seed grows 'true' to type and can be saved

ORGANIC
Does not contain any genetically engineered traits, grown in conformity with strict standards

HYBRID (F1)
Seed created by cross-breeding two different plants. Uniform crop and disease-resistance

GMO
The seed's genetics have been altered by biotechnology to give it particular traits

HEIRLOOM
A heritage/heirloom, historic variety, which has fallen out of favour in commercial production

AGM
Has received the Royal Horticultural Society (RHS) Award of Garden Merit (AGM)

Germination

When warmth, water and oxygen become available, a seed's coat swells and breaks open. If you watch your seedlings closely, you'll notice there are two ways in which they emerge from the soil.

EPIGEAL GROWTH
Plants such as French beans and onions

HYPOGEAL GROWTH
Plants such as peas and runner beans

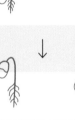

When some seeds grow, part of their embryo morphs to form the plant's first leaves. These are known as 'seed leaves'

Some seeds germinate leaving the seed's food stores below ground, feeding the plant as it grows above ground

Seed leaves emerge above ground, feeding the plant with nutrients stored in the seed

This makes the plant less susceptible to frost and pests, and enables it to grow in nutrient-poor soil

Then the growing shoot emerges. It will grow branches and leaves

The growing shoot emerges from the soil; at first it's curved to protect the tip, then it straightens out

Seed leaves become green and photosynthetic. First foliage appears. The seedling is now a plant

The first leaves to appear are 'true' photosynthetic leaves, not seed leaves

Sowing seeds

How, where and when you raise seeds depends on the variety and its specific climatic needs. Seed packets help guide you as to which of these growing methods you need to adopt.

Indoors

Starting seeds indoors creates a longer growing season because you can sow while waiting for the weather to warm up. It also offers protection and a controlled environment – especially heat. Get seeds going indoors ('under cover') by sowing seeds into a pot or tray. Then 'transplant' seeds to their final growing location later on.

 WINDOWSILL: Offers a warm, sunny spot for a plant's early life

 PROPAGATOR: Heated or unheated – can provide a moist, warm, consistent environment

Outdoors

Sowing seeds 'directly' outside, where they grow to full-size plants, is more straightforward but your seeds (and young seedlings) are exposed to changes in the weather and to mice and birds. However, some crops, like carrots, dislike being moved – so for them, this method is the best option. Avoid growing frost-tender plants outdoors until risk of frost has passed.

SOWING IN ROWS: Sowing in straight rows makes weeding easier later on. Use string as a guide if you want to make precise rows.

 BROADCAST SOWING: Prepare the soil, then throw handfuls of seed over the area – not advisable on a windy day!

Sowing technique

Seeds should be sown thinly and evenly. Don't tip seeds straight from the packet; instead, pour a small amount into the fold crease of your palm. Pinch larger seeds from your palm and sprinkle. Scatter very small seed, like lettuce. Or, to help sow small seed evenly, mix with sand before scattering.

Potting on

Seedlings must be moved into bigger pots when they outgrow their first home. This is known as 'potting on'. It is undertaken when 'true' leaves have developed, roots have emerged and the plant is large enough to handle.

Pricking out

Removing seedlings from pots is called 'pricking out'. Never handle a seedling by its delicate stem. Instead, hold it by a leaf and support the weight of the roots with a pencil as you lift it. Damaged leaves usually grow back; stem damage is more serious.

⊕ Know how – Hardening off

Any plant raised indoors may go into shock if it is suddenly confronted with a changeable climate outside. Plants must be introduced to the outside world gently, through a process known as 'hardening off'. Do this over three weeks. Place plants in a sheltered position in front of a south-facing wall or hedge and cover with a double layer of fleece. Bring inside at night for one week. During the second week, remove a layer of fleece. By week three, remove the other layer of fleece during the day, and leave plants outside at night.

Watering essentials

Water is key for growing crops but it is tricky to judge how much water to give them. Largely, this is because plants vary in how thirsty they are. The rate at which they absorb water also depends on how fast a plant is growing.

METAL CAN
Galvanized, traditional, sturdy and long-lasting

LONG-REACH
Its long neck is handy for difficult-to-reach containers

SPRAY BOTTLE
For keeping seedlings moist and for misting plants

When and how to water

Work a spade into your plot, around 30cm (12in) deep. If the blade comes out dry when you remove it, it's time to get the watering can out. Containers require vigilance; they dry out quicker than soil in open ground and plant roots cannot branch out to seek moisture elsewhere. You can test the soil in containers by sticking your finger under the surface to see if the soil is dry, or simply by picking the container up – if the plant is in need of water, the container will feel light.

Do not water foliage but aim water around the base of plants to direct it to the roots. Water in the morning, before the sun evaporates your efforts, or early evening (although plants sitting in cold water can attract slugs and snails overnight). To retain moisture and control weeds, which steal water from your crops, apply a layer of mulch.

Most veg need moist soil. But they vary in the amount of water they need, and at which stage they need it most – this is known as the 'critical watering period'.

The right amount of water

Light, frequent sprinklings will not reach the roots where the water is needed and will readily evaporate into the air

Instead, give plants a decent soaking but less often – once or twice a week for many plants

Exceptions to this rule are seedlings. Keep soil moist with a spray bottle or by standing pots in trays of water

Bottle-drip irrigation

Use a flowerpot or PET plastic bottle with holes punched in the bottom. Bury it in the soil alongside a plant, and fill with water. Water will slowly soak into the soil, direct to the roots where it is most needed, avoiding waste.

Water butts

Rainwater is free yet most ends up heading straight down the drain. However, water butts capture and store rainwater for future use. Fit a lid over the top to stop animals getting inside. Connect to the downpipe from your guttering, using a connection kit. Fit a tap at the bottom or scoop your watering can into the butt from above.

Cultivating your soil

Digging is undertaken to improve the structure and condition of the soil. This is done in autumn or spring, when the earth is moist but not sodden.

Double digging

In autumn, mark out your area for cultivation. Begin at one end, digging out a 60cm (2ft) wide 'slice' of earth, to the depth of your spade blade. Move this topsoil to the opposite end of your plot.

Push a fork into the soil to the depth of the fork. Break up the soil by twisting and turning the fork. Leave this layer of soil in place. Add organic matter and mix and mash in.

Repeat, digging out another 60cm (2ft) slice next door to your first trench. Put the topsoil of the second slice into the first trench, filling it back up to ground level or thereabouts.

Do this until you have reached the final portion of your plot. Fill this empty trench with the topsoil from the first trench. Leave the plot to settle over winter.

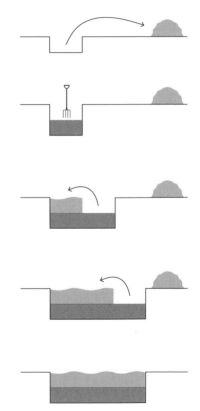

No-dig method

'No-dig' is a cultivation method in which you lay large amounts of organic matter on top of the soil and simply let worms and other organisms 'dig' the ground for you.

A lasagne garden

Lasagne gardening is one type of no-dig method. Also called 'sheet composting', organic materials are layered one on top of another, much like lasagne.

First, cut down any larger weeds. Then add several layers of newspaper or thick cardboard to smother grass and weed seeds. Water. Next, lay down 10–20cm (4–8in) of woody 'brown' material, such as branches and twigs.

Add several more layers on top, alternating 'green' layers of semi-rotted leaves, rotted manure, garden compost, grass clippings and veg peelings with 'brown' dry layers. Repeat until the 'lasagne' is around 50cm (20in) high.

Sprinkle compost over the top, and it's ready to plant with seeds.

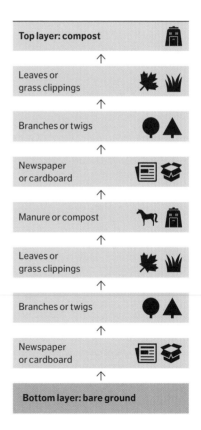

Top layer: compost

↑

Leaves or grass clippings

↑

Branches or twigs

↑

Newspaper or cardboard

↑

Manure or compost

↑

Leaves or grass clippings

↑

Branches or twigs

↑

Newspaper or cardboard

↑

Bottom layer: bare ground

Caring for your soil

Growing the same veg in the same section of ground, season after season, exhausts the soil of nutrients and contributes to the build-up of diseases.

Vegetable plants make their mark on the soil. Certain plants build fertility in the soil, while others deplete it. This is the principle behind crop rotation, which organic growers use to keep soil healthy, support strong crops and control pests and diseases.

To adopt this practice in your own garden, place vegetable plants with high nutrient demands – such as potatoes and cabbage – where less demanding crops, such as carrots and onions, have grown the previous season.

$\rightarrow$ Know how – Green manure

Green manures are plants grown specifically to build soil fertility. You might grow them when your plot is bare during winter, to prevent the nutrient loss and soil erosion that happens during these periods. Or you can also use them to 'fix' nitrogen in the soil.

Sow green manures in rows or broadcast-sow them across the soil. When you need the plot again, chop the foliage down and leave it to wilt, then dig it into the topsoil. Leave for two weeks before planting seeds.

Try winter field bean (*Vicia faba*), which is a legume for heavy soils, and phacelia (*Phacelia tanacetifolia*), which improves soil structure – its flowers are also fantastic for bees and butterflies.

Crop rotation: a four-year plan

Draw up a four-year plan, starting by dividing the veg you want to grow into groups. Next, divide the plot into mini beds – you need at least three beds to make it work. Move each group forward into a new mini bed every year.

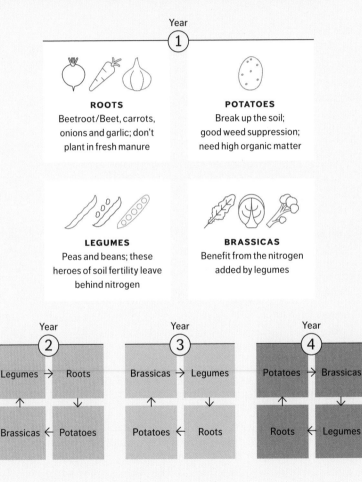

Year
(1)

ROOTS
Beetroot/Beet, carrots, onions and garlic; don't plant in fresh manure

POTATOES
Break up the soil; good weed suppression; need high organic matter

LEGUMES
Peas and beans; these heroes of soil fertility leave behind nitrogen

BRASSICAS
Benefit from the nitrogen added by legumes

Year
(2)

Legumes → Roots

↑   ↓

Brassicas ← Potatoes

Year
(3)

Brassicas → Legumes

↑   ↓

Potatoes ← Roots

Year
(4)

Potatoes → Brassicas

↑   ↓

Roots ← Legumes

Designing a polyculture plot

Planting clever combinations of vegetables enables crops to support one another, rather than compete, and leads to fewer pests and diseases.

Principles of polyculture

While monoculture is a system of growing single crops in rows or patches, polyculture approaches gardening more holistically. A polyculture plot mimics a forest. It has a plant canopy, an understorey, groundcover and climbing plants – this creates a diverse and beautiful ecosystem.

Polyculture works by combining vegetable plants so they can be mutually beneficial, or so they can support one another.

⊘ Know how – Planting for polyculture

Sow large seeds, like peas and beans, at their usual spacing and scatter medium-sized seeds, like beet, spinach, chard and radish, or sow these in clumps. Small seeds like lettuce, onion and carrot can be sown individually and thinly across the bed. Next, sow groundcover such as mustard or rocket/arugula at the end.

 → →

Peas and beans   Beetroot/beet, radishes, spinach and chard   Carrots and lettuce   Rocket/arugula or mustard

Plant companion plants, such as marigolds, basil and comfrey around the edge of the bed. Cover with mulch and water. After three months, you will have harvested the groundcover. Large plants remain and will keep cropping until the autumn or winter.

Companion planting

Plants can make great partners for one another, protecting their mates from pests and improving the chances of pollination. Here are a few pairings you might try.

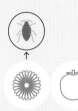

Plant tomatoes with marigolds: The smell of marigolds repels greenfly and blackfly

Plant summer savory and broad beans/fava beans: Savory protects beans from black bean aphid

Scatter mint leaves across the bed: They can repel an ant infestation

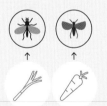

Plant carrots with leeks: Leeks deter carrot fly, while carrots repel onion fly and leek moth

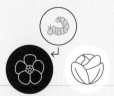

Plant nasturtiums with cabbage: Caterpillars will lay eggs on nasturtiums instead of on cabbages

Plant basil: Attracts whitefly, hence acts as a sacrificial plant, protecting other plants

Stocking your shed

There are countless products designed for gardeners, so it can be really confusing to work out what is truly necessary, particularly if you are starting from scratch.

What are tools for?

Heavy work

SPADE: For digging and turning over soil

FORK: For tilling large areas and breaking up compacted soil

MATTOCK: For breaking up compacted clay

AZADA: Useful for clearing ground

HOE: Long-handled for removing weeds

SOIL RAKE: For hard landscaping, to loosen and level soil

GRASS RAKE: Flexible for collecting grass

Cutting & pruning

SECATEURS: For cutting thin branches

SHEARS: For cutting and shaping hedges and shrubs

TRUG: For collecting fruit and veg

Hand tools

HAND FORK: For cultivating, weeding or aerating small areas

TROWEL: For digging small planting holes

HAND HOE: For weeding raised beds

MARKERS: To mark, name and date plants

Miscellaneous

DIBBER: To make precise planting holes

STRING: For marking out sowing rows

GLOVES: To protect hands, especially from thorns

WATERING CAN: Less wasteful than a hose, particularly if fitted with a fine rose

WHEELBARROW: For carrying heavy loads of soil and mulch

BUCKET: For storing pruned foliage or other material for the compost bin

Dibber

Shears

Trowel

String

Secateurs

Markers

Hand fork

Gloves

Fork

Hoe

Grass rake

Bucket

Hand hoe

Spade

Soil rake

Azada

Watering can

Trug

Wheelbarrow

Things to grow

- Leafy & salad vegetables
- Western brassicas
- Flowering & fruiting vegetables
- Podded vegetables
- Bulb & stem vegetables
- Root & tuberous vegetables
- Herbs & edible flowers

Nurturing any plant from seed is a rewarding venture, but all the more so when you can taste the results. From crunchy cucamelons, to nutty sprouts, spicy radishes to the sweetest corn, these guides provide simple instructions on how to harvest some spectacular crops with minimal fuss.

Leafy & salad vegetables

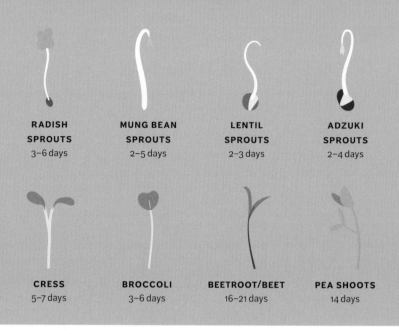

RADISH SPROUTS
3–6 days

MUNG BEAN SPROUTS
2–5 days

LENTIL SPROUTS
2–3 days

ADZUKI SPROUTS
2–4 days

CRESS
5–7 days

BROCCOLI
3–6 days

BEETROOT/BEET
16–21 days

PEA SHOOTS
14 days

Microgreens

From seed to sprout, microgreens are ready in a matter of days

GROWING CALENDAR
Sow all year round

Microgreens are quick-growing plants that can be raised indoors all year round. These leafy veg are the young shoots of common salad plants and herbs that have been harvested very early, soon after they've produced their first leaves.

A sunny windowsill and a seed tray are all you need. You could use recycled take-away food cartons, yoghurt pots or even eggshells. Or you could buy a special sprouting jar.

Rich in vitamins and minerals, and intense in flavour, microgreens prove that big doesn't necessarily mean better.

⊕ Know how – Buying seeds

The seeds used to grow microgreens are the same as for full-size vegetables, salads and herbs. Or try reduced-price, end-of-season seeds of anything that grows an edible leaf (basil, leeks, radish, chard, kale). But for best results, buy special sprouting seeds.

Sow

Seed sprouts

Soak a large handful of seeds in water overnight, then drain. Place a few sheets of kitchen roll in your seed tray. Dampen the kitchen roll well and pour out excess water. Sprinkle seeds across the surface.

Alternatively, put your soaked seeds in a sprouting jar and rinse twice a day. Place on a warm windowsill and mist daily. Your sprouts will be ready to harvest in a few days.

Microgreens

Fill a shallow tray, at least 5cm (2in) deep and with drainage holes in the bottom, with a layer of compost. Sprinkle your seeds over the soil, about 5mm (¼in) apart – you'll need fewer seeds than for sprouts.

Cover with a 5mm (¼in) layer of compost and water. Keep in a sunny spot indoors. Mist to keep the soil moist but not wet. No additional feed is required. When the leaves are 2–3cm (¾–1¼in) high, you can begin harvesting by cutting the top of the plants as required, leaving some leaves to grow as cut-and-come-again veg.

Eat

Microgreens are at their best consumed immediately. Combine with grated carrots, avocado, cubed beetroot and sunflower seeds to make a highly virtuous summer salad.

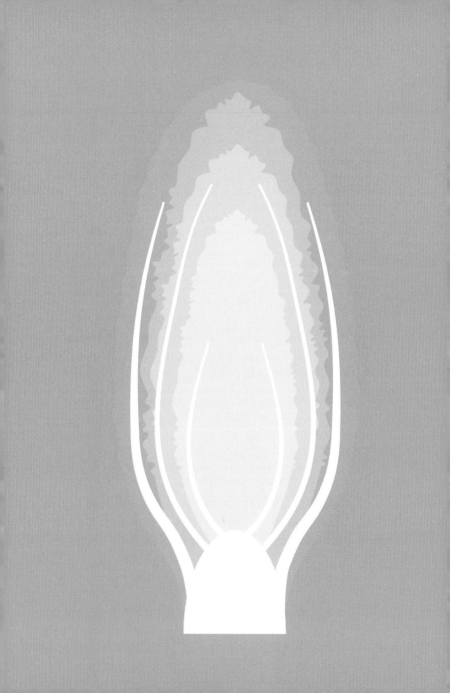

Salad leaves

SEEDS
Storage: up to 3 years
Germination: 6–12 days

POT STARS
Grow several varieties
together in 15–30cm
(6–12in) pots

GOOD COMPANIONS
Radish, beetroot, carrots,
strawberries

Growing salad leaves close to the kitchen table simple makes sense. Ready-to-eat bagged leaves from the supermarket contain far fewer nutrients. And then there's the waste: rare is the person who has never chucked a limp, neglected iceberg lettuce in the bin.

Homegrown salad leaves can be picked whenever needed and cost a fraction of the price of their shop-bought peers. Homegrown produce is fresher, healthier and better for the planet.

Salad leaves are also easy to cultivate in the tiniest gardens. They will grow rapidly in any small space as well as in window boxes 10cm (4in) deep. You can begin enjoying your efforts just eight weeks after sowing.

Growing calendar

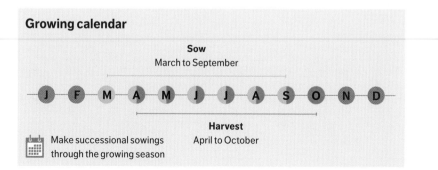

Sow
March to September

J F M A M J J A S O N D

Harvest
April to October

Make successional sowings
through the growing season

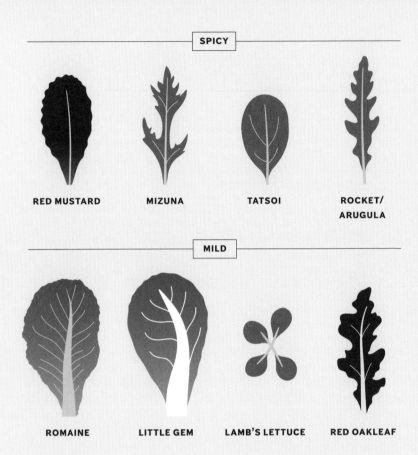

RED MUSTARD **MIZUNA** **TATSOI** **ROCKET/ ARUGULA**

MILD

ROMAINE **LITTLE GEM** **LAMB'S LETTUCE** **RED OAKLEAF**

Varieties

Get creative with salad leaves in a range of tastes, textures and colours. Salad leaf mixes offer variety and require little effort. Look for mixed packets such as 'Oriental Saladini', containing mizuna, red mustard and pak choi, or 'Misticanza', which includes loose-leaved salad leaves like chicory, rocket and watercress. Or make your own salad leaf seed mix.

Sow

Sow in a pot
Fill a container with peat-free compost. Water the soil, and then scatter seeds on top. Cover with a thin layer of compost. Sow a new batch of lettuce seeds each week for a constant supply of seedlings ready to plant out. Keep seeds well watered.

Sow directly outdoors
Ensure your plot has been conditioned with organic matter, garden compost or well-rotted manure. Create a shallow drill, at a depth of around 1cm (½in) and with 10–15cm (4–6in) between rows. Water the bottom of the drill before you sow. Sow in rows and cover with a little more soil or compost.

Grow

Salad leaves need water to grow – lettuce can bolt in hot weather, so water them when the soil is dry and keep weeds at bay.

Harvest & eat

With mixed lettuces, some varieties can take over, so harvest the dominant crops first. Loose-leaf salad leaves can be grown as a cut-and-come-again crop. Simply cut leaves when plants are 5–10cm (2–4in) tall. Water the plants and more leaves will sprout, possibly as many as three times.

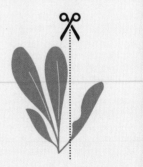

For heading varieties, such as iceberg, wait until the plant has reached full size and then harvest whole, by cutting at the base.

For repeat crops, add spent compost from containers to the ground before sowing.

Spinach

Spinacia oleracea

SEEDS

Storage: up to 3 years
Germination: 12–24 days

POT STARS

Try Spinach 'Apollo'

GOOD COMPANIONS

Strawberries, beans, peas

One of the most nutrient-rich vegetables around, spinach packs a powerful antioxidant punch. Grow your own and you'll have a fantastically healthy glut of greens all year: spinach is available in both winter and summer varieties.

There are three different types; savoy has crisp, creased, curly leaves that possess a springy texture; smooth-leaf has flat, unwrinkled, spade-shaped leaves; and semi-savoy, which is similar in texture to savoy, but does not have as crinkled an appearance.

These plants benefit from rich soil and water in dry weather. Spinach can be difficult to grow as it is prone to bolting in hot weather and can be beset by pests. For an alternative, try a spinach-like substitute (see p.56).

Growing calendar

Sow summer spinach
March to May

Harvest
May to October

Next year

J F M A M J J A S O N D J F M A

Sow winter spinach
July to September

Harvest
October to April

Not 'true' spinach but grown in the same way

PERPETUAL
Sow in the spring
and harvest through
the year – and even
into the next

NEW ZEALAND
A low-maintenance,
attractive foliage
plant that stays
productive
throughout summer

TREE SPINACH
Edible young leaves
are bright pink,
turning green later in
the summer; needs
plenty of room

Sow

Sow in a border, raised bed or pot
All spinach, true or not, is started off in
a similar way.

In spring, prep the border or raised bed by
removing stones and weeds, and digging in well-rotted manure. This organic
matter prevents leaves from turning bitter. Sow seeds 2cm (¾in) deep in rows
30cm (12in) apart. New Zealand and tree spinach need more space, so keep
about 60cm (2ft) apart.

For pot-grown spinach, fill a 15–20cm (6–8in) pot with compost. Leave at
least 7.5cm (3in) of space between each seed. The more space you allow each
plant, the bigger the leaves will grow.

Grow

When the seedlings are 2cm (¾in) tall, thin them to remove weaker plants
and use the thinnings as microgreens (see pp.48–49).

True spinach needs the most care, especially regular watering in summer to
stop it from bolting.

Tree spinach can accumulate nitrogen, which is not good when eaten in
large quantities, so it's best not to plant it on recently manured soils or feed it
manufactured fertilizer.

Harvest

Regular picking encourages new
leaf growth. Pick summer sowings
between late May and the end
of October. Pick winter cultivars
between October and April.

Spinach may
be grown as a cut-
and-come-again
crop for use in
salads

Summer varieties of spinach tend to run to seed fairly quickly, especially in
hot, dry summers. So harvest leaves young and make successional sowings
every few weeks for a constant supply.

Winter varieties provide leaves for a longer period, though they soon run to
seed when the weather warms up.

Store

Spinach can be stored for up to three weeks if washed, dried and kept in
plastic containers in the fridge. Leaves can also be frozen.

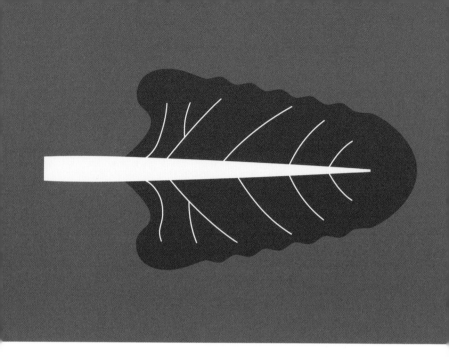

Chard

Beta vulgaris

SEEDS
Storage: up to 4 years
Germination: 10–14 days

GROWING CALENDAR
Sow late spring and
late summer. Harvest
throughout year

GOOD COMPANIONS
Strawberries, beans, peas

Chard, or leaf beet, has a long season. This leafy veg is tough, with the ability to survive winter frosts and produce yields right up to the following spring. Make two sowings a year (in late spring and late summer), and you'll have homegrown chard all the year through. With wide, fan-like leaves and crunchy stalks, it is really two tasty vegetables in one plant.

Striking leaf stalks (which can be red, gold, yellow, striped or white) make chard a beautiful ornamental plant. And it's perfectly content in a container.

Sow

Sow directly outdoors
Ensure your soil is rich and slightly acidic. Poorly conditioned soil will result in tough, stringy stalks. Always add well-rotted compost before planting to prevent this. Plant into 1cm (½in) deep holes, with a space of 45cm (18in) between rows.

Varieties
White-stemmed 'Monstruoso' and 'Large White Ribbed' are among the easiest of varieties for gardeners, as they are less likely to go to seed after cold snaps. Red varieties are more of a challenge for beginner gardeners, but for taste, productivity and looks, try 'Pink Passion'.

Grow

Thin out the seedlings when they are large enough to handle to one plant every 30cm (12in) and use the thinnings as microgreens (see pp.48–49). Mulch when the soil is warm and moist, and keep watered.

Feed with an organic, high-nitrogen fertilizer once the plants are around 15cm (6in) tall. Water well and keep the soil evenly moist, particularly in hot spells, to avoid bolting. Good moisture and air circulation will help prevent common chard problems, such as downy mildew.

Harvest

Treat as a cut-and-come-again crop any time from when plants reach 5cm (2in) tall. Picking young leaves encourages more growth. Cut the outer leaves first, then work inwards. Carefully pick them off (don't pull up the roots by tugging too hard). Or you can leave the plants to grow to full size.

Western brassicas

Varieties

An amazing number of vegetables we know and love today, originated from *Brassica oleracea* – a plant of coastal cliffs.

Wild cabbage
Brassica oleracea

The cabbage family has a very long history, being first grown for food around 2,000 years ago. Thanks to farmers and gardeners saving seeds from those cabbage plants that had interesting or useful characteristics, eight major groups of vegetables we eat today have been created from just one plant.

Cauliflower: Its name translates as 'stalk flower', a nod to its place in a family of plants mainly grown for their edible leaves.

Broccoli: Related to cauliflower, it is grown for its clusters of unopened flower buds and tender flower stalks. (See pp.72–75.)

Cabbage: Can be wrinkled-leafed, smooth-leafed, white, red, green, or pointy.

Brussels sprouts: Grown for the miniature heads (sprouts) which develop in the axils of the leaves. (See pp.68–71.)

Kale: A leafy, non-heading cabbage that's retained its primitive form over thousands of years. (See pp.64–67.)

Kohlrabi: Grown for its edible leaves and large bulb, which resembles a turnip.

Kale

Brassica oleracea var. *sabellica*

SEEDS
Storage: up to 4 years
Germination: 7–12 days

POT STARS
'Red Russian'

GOOD COMPANIONS
Grow near beetroots,
potatoes, celery and
rosemary

A low-maintenance, cool-weather veg that's harvested for its edible leaves, kale has been enjoying a revival.

This brassica, which is very similar in appearance to wild cabbage, grows in most soils, will tolerate some shade and is extremely hardy. In fact, its flavour improves once plants are 'kissed' by frost.

Kale attracts very few pests compared with cauliflower and cabbage. If you're short of space, you can plant kale in ground that you've already used for potatoes or peas, or in a container, where it will be happy as long as you move it to a shady spot during the summer.

Varieties
Foliage can be green, red or purple, and cultivars with coloured leaves are sometimes grown as ornamental plants. Varieties of kale are grouped according to leaf type (see p.66).

Growing calendar

Sow indoors
April to May

Plant out
June to July

Next year

J F M A M J J A S O N D J F M

Sow outdoors
June to August

Harvest
October to March

CURLY
Tight, ruffled crinkled leaves in bright or dark green, or purple. Pungent, peppery flavour. Try 'Westland Autumn'

CAVOLO NERO
Also known as black kale, lacinato kale and dinosaur kale, thanks to its bubble-effect leaves. Tastes nutty and sweet

PLAIN-LEAVED
Open-shaped leaves and edible spring shoots. Try 'Cottagers' and 'Thousand Head'

RAPE KALE
Pick shoots from Feb–May. Try 'Ragged Jack', 'Hungry Gap' and 'Asparagus Kale'

LEAF AND SPEAR
Cross between curly-leaved and plain-leaved. Try 'Pentland Brig'

Sow

Start off in seed or module trays
In late April, sow a few seeds in a module tray or seed tray. Sow 1cm (½in) deep. Keep in a bright but cool position. Don't allow them to dry out.

Once they have germinated, remove the weakest seedlings and leave the strongest. Keep the compost moist. Seedlings will be ready to plant out after approx. six weeks, when they have four or five leaves and are 10cm (4in) tall. Harden off.

Grow

Add some organic fertilizer to the soil. Carefully lift the seedlings, taking care not to damage the roots. Space them about 30cm (12in) apart in rows 45–60cm (18–24in) apart. Larger-growing varieties may need up to 50cm (20in) between each plant. Plant so that the lowest set of leaves is sitting on the soil surface. Firm the soil around the seedlings with your foot and water thoroughly. Protect with netting.

Water, mulch, and feed in spring. Moist soil helps keep the leaves crisp and sweet. Remove any yellowing leaves. Caterpillars and cutworms enjoy nibbling at kale but it's largely problem-free. If your kale is tall, stake it to give support.

Kales are a very hardy veg, some surviving temperatures of -15°C (5°F)

Harvest

Pick little and often. Start harvesting the leaves from October. Start with the outer leaves from the top of the plant (the 'crown'). This will prompt sideshoot growth, which will be ready between February and May and can be picked when they're around 10cm (4in) long.

If you prefer a cut-and-come-again crop, harvest leaves when plants are 5cm (2in) high. Young leaves will continue to be produced after that.

Eat

CRISPS: To make the perfect kale crisps, harvest three to four large handfuls of black kale, strip the leaves from the stems, wash well and dry. Mix salt and paprika, and massage into the kale leaves, along with 1 tbsp of extra-virgin olive oil. Spread on two trays lined with baking parchment and cook for 15–20 minutes at 150°C (300°F/Gas 2) until crispy around the edges.

Store

Eat as soon as possible after harvesting. Leaves picked after frost are the tastiest. The leaves can be stored in the fridge for a week in a plastic bag. Tender shoots can be frozen, but blanch them first.

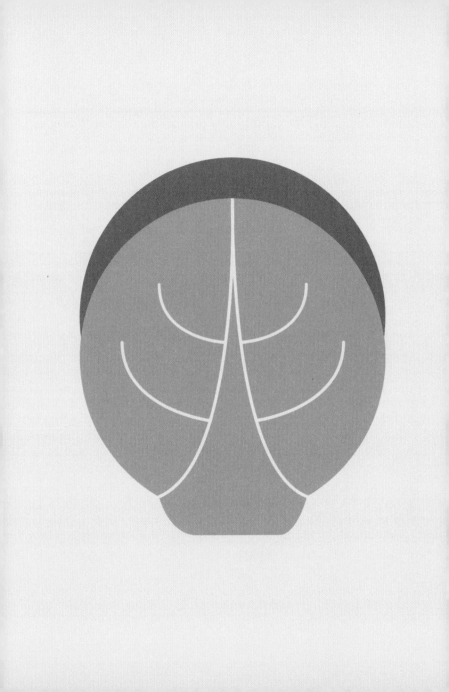

Brussels sprouts

Brassica oleracea var. *gemmifera*

SEEDS
Storage: up to 4 years
Germination: 7–12 days

POT STARS
Minimum 30cm (12in)
One plant per pot

GOOD COMPANIONS
Grow near sage,
cucumbers and chard

Over-boiled Christmas sprouts have given this plucky little brassica a bad reputation. But cooked with love and care, Brussels sprouts can be delicious and tender, sweet and nutty. Believe it or not, they also taste great raw.

These miniature cabbages are a slow-growing crop, with a growing season that spans 100 days.

Planted in spring, sprout buds first begin to form halfway into their growing cycle. Sprouts form at the base first, then progressively higher up the central stem, culminating in a cabbage-like top.

Harvest in winter, usually after the first frost. But if you're planning on freezing your sprouts, pick them before the leaves become damaged by the cold.

Growing calendar

Sow indoors
March to April

Next year

J F M A M J J A S O N D J F M

Plant out
May to June

Harvest
October to March

Varieties

Varieties are classed according to their time of maturity as early, mid-season or late, with the latter being the hardiest. Try 'Abacus' for early crops of dark green sprouts, 'Maximus' for a mid-season crop and 'Revenge' for a very late-season sprout, which produces high yields of nutty, easy-to-pick veg.

Sow

Start off in seed trays
Prepare the sprouts' final seedbed in the autumn or winter before sowing, ideally in a spot where peas or beans have been grown previously. Ensure it is sheltered from strong winds. Dig in plenty of organic matter or well-rotted manure. Leave to settle over winter.

Start your sprouts off in seed trays in March and April. Place inside a plastic bag until germination, then grow in a cool spot.

Grow

In May to June, when seedlings are 10–15cm (4–6in) high and have seven true leaves, they are ready to be grown on in a border or raised bed. Harden off. Water seedlings before moving them and rake over the plot.

Create a hole and plant in firmly, with the lowest leaves just above the surface of the soil giving each seedling 60–70cm (24–28in) of space both between plants and between rows.

Water again once seedlings are in the ground. Water every 10–14 days in dry weather, and a few weeks before harvest apply a single heavy watering if the weather is very dry. Apply a top dressing of liquid comfrey around each plant in July. Earth up (see p.168) in autumn to support the growing plants.

Protect from pests with fine netting. Pick off any slugs or cabbage white caterpillars.

Harvest

Sprouts that are ready to harvest should be firm, closed and about the size of a walnut.

Harvest sprouts from the lower part of the stem first, cutting them off with a sharp knife and working steadily up the stem. Cut off yellow leaves and any open sprouts – these can go in the compost bin.

Wide spacing on plants encourages good air circulation, which keeps plants disease-free

Eat

Sprout tops are edible cut-and-come-again greens. Or you can eat them raw in salads – they're delicious served with apples and walnuts.

You could also try them roasted in olive oil with Parmesan cheese, chilli flakes and lemon zest.

Store

You can lift an entire plant with the sprouts still attached to the stem, which keeps them fresh before cooking. Keep them in a cool, frost-free place. Store fresh, unwashed sprouts in plastic bags in the fridge.

Sprouting broccoli

Brassica oleracea var. *italica*

SEEDS

Storage: up to 3 years
Germination: 7–12 days

GOOD COMPANIONS

Nasturtiums will deter cabbage white butterflies. Don't plant where other brassicas have been in the past four years

Taking between nine months and a year to mature, it is natural to question why this veg is worth the effort.

Firstly, freshness is crucial with sprouting broccoli, so this is a top reason to grow your own. In contrast to modern heading broccoli, sprouting broccoli produces many smaller shoots with small 'broccoli heads' or florets. Those sweet, vivid florets make this veg perhaps the most visually pleasing of the brassicas you could grow.

Just remember to plant your sprouting broccoli in a position where you can leave it be for a long while. Avoid planting in shallow and sandy soils and in any spot that's exposed to strong winds.

Growing calendar

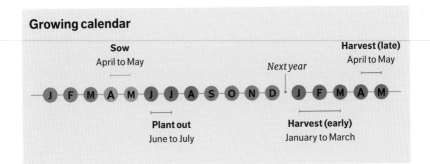

Sow
April to May

Next year

Harvest (late)
April to May

J F M A M J J A S O N D J F M A M

Plant out
June to July

Harvest (early)
January to March

73

Varieties

Sprouting broccoli comes in two colours – purple and white. And there are early and late varieties of each, so check which you are buying. For a faster-growing crop, try the green Calabrese varieties, which are harvested in the summer or autumn.

SPROUTING BROCCOLI TYPES

PURPLE SPROUTING
Sweet and extremely hardy; needs the cold winter weather to form the florets

WHITE SPROUTING
White types are even more delicate in flavour

Sow

Sow directly outdoors

Pick a spot in the garden that is sheltered from the wind and where other brassicas have not been growing for the last two years. Prep this plot in the autumn. Ensure the soil is rich by adding organic matter or well-rotted manure. As with all brassicas, lime the soil in winter if required.

Start the seeds in a seedbed in late spring at a depth of 1cm (½in) and spaced 30cm (12in) apart. Keep the soil moist to hasten germination.

In early summer, when seedlings are around 7.5cm (3in) high and have four or five leaves, you can transplant them to their final growing position.

Grow

Plant the seedlings a little deeper than they were in the seedbed, with around 60cm (2ft) between plants and a similar distance between rows. Water thoroughly after planting. Cover with netting to protect from pests.

Water weekly, and once a few weeks before harvest in very dry conditions. Hoe to prevent weeds from establishing. Remove any yellow leaves. Apply high-nitrogen organic feed when the plants are 20cm (8in) tall. Stake in autumn if necessary. Add a layer of compost to feed the plants and give the roots some protection from frost.

Harvest

Harvest little and often to encourage more growth. But pick the central stem first to encourage more growth. Plants may crop for two months. If left unpicked, the buds will flower (bolt) and that will be the end of your harvest. On the other hand, the flowers are good for bees.

Pick the spears before the buds have opened

Eat

Steam for the best flavour. Pair with anchovies and coat with a dressing, or cover in a Parmesan herb crumb.

Store

Will keep for a few days in an airtight bag in the fridge. To freeze, soak in salted water for 15 minutes, then rinse and dry. Blanch for 3–4 minutes, then freeze.

Flowering & fruiting vegetables

Chillies

Capsicum spp.

SEEDS
Storage: up to 5 years
Germination: 7–12 days

POT STARS
Grow one plant in a 30cm
(12in) container

GOOD COMPANIONS
Grow with basil, tomatoes,
squash and rosemary.
Geraniums deter
chilli pests

Chillies are now more popular than the large, sweet peppers for garden growing, as our palates have become increasingly accustomed to hot flavours.

Grow your own chillies, choosing from a range of shapes, colours and heat – from cultivars that give a delicate tingle to those with scorching firepower.

It is a chemical compound in the chilli – capsaicin – that stimulates the nerve endings in the mouth, skin and eyes. So the more capsaicin a chilli has, the hotter it is. This pungency is measured according to Scoville heat units (SHU) (see p.80).

Small plants are perfect in pots for small, sunny gardens. You can also grow your own chilli farm in rows on a vegetable patch. This plant loves sun and heat, and is pollinated by bees.

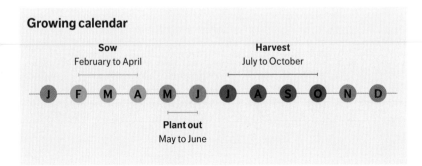

Growing calendar

Sow
February to April

Harvest
July to October

J F M A M J J A S O N D

Plant out
May to June

Scoville scale

The Scoville scale is a measure of the 'hotness' of a chilli pepper, or anything derived from chilli peppers.

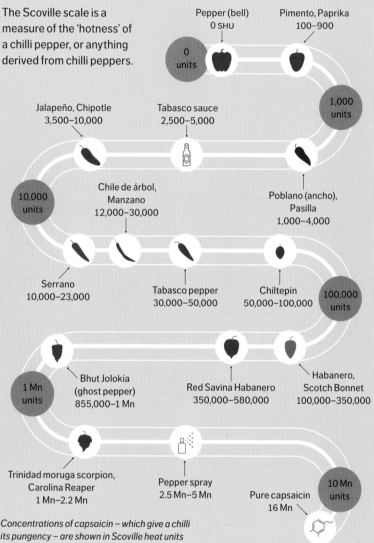

Pepper (bell)
0 SHU

Pimento, Paprika
100–900

0 units

1,000 units

Jalapeño, Chipotle
3,500–10,000

Tabasco sauce
2,500–5,000

Poblano (ancho),
Pasilla
1,000–4,000

Chile de árbol,
Manzano
12,000–30,000

10,000 units

Serrano
10,000–23,000

Tabasco pepper
30,000–50,000

Chiltepin
50,000–100,000

100,000 units

1 Mn units

Bhut Jolokia
(ghost pepper)
855,000–1 Mn

Red Savina Habanero
350,000–580,000

Habanero,
Scotch Bonnet
100,000–350,000

Trinidad moruga scorpion,
Carolina Reaper
1 Mn–2.2 Mn

Pepper spray
2.5 Mn–5 Mn

Pure capsaicin
16 Mn

10 Mn units

Concentrations of capsaicin – which give a chilli its pungency – are shown in Scoville heat units 1 Mn = 1 million

80

Varieties

There is a chilli cultivar to suit every palate and cuisine, so have fun and experiment. Try growing 'Caribbean Antillais' for its small, aromatic fruits or 'Fiesta', an ornamental plant whose fruits are very hot indeed. 'Demon Red' produces upward-pointing, bright red fruit that are used in Thai cooking.

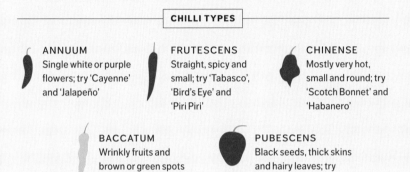

CHILLI TYPES

ANNUUM
Single white or purple flowers; try 'Cayenne' and 'Jalapeño'

FRUTESCENS
Straight, spicy and small; try 'Tabasco', 'Bird's Eye' and 'Piri Piri'

CHINENSE
Mostly very hot, small and round; try 'Scotch Bonnet' and 'Habanero'

BACCATUM
Wrinkly fruits and brown or green spots on flower petals; try 'Aji'

PUBESCENS
Black seeds, thick skins and hairy leaves; try 'Rocoto'

Sow

Start off in pots or module trays

Sow two seeds in 9cm (3½in) pots filled with compost. Cover with a clear plastic bag and place on a warm, sunny windowsill or in an airing cupboard. Keep soil moist but not soaking wet. If you have room for lots of plants, then start the seeds in a seed tray. Transplant seedlings to small pots once they've germinated. Remove any weaker plants at this stage. Once again, place a clear plastic bag over the pot or tray. Continue to grow indoors, in a warm spot. Water every other day, or enough so that pots do not dry out.

Grow

Chillies should be moved to bigger pots once the seedlings are about 10cm (4in) tall – they will stop growing if not transplanted. Use 30cm (12in) pots, opting for dark-coloured pots as these are better at retaining heat. Place in a sunny, warm spot – a mini greenhouse is best as this provides the warmth that chilli plants crave.

Keep watering to stop the plants drying out but don't let the soil get waterlogged. Misting plants, especially greenhouse plants, with a water bottle will help the fruit set and keeps red spider mite away. Feed with an organic fertilizer, such as kelp meal, when the first flowers appear.

(→) Know how – Growing chilli plants outdoors

Whether planting in large pots, growbags or into the ground, chilli plants need heat and will produce more fruit under cover. This could be provided by a mini greenhouse, a polytunnel or a cloche. However, given a decent summer, most plants will do fine outside.

If you decide to plant your chillies outdoors, you'll need a mild climate. You must also harden them off first (see p.33). After several weeks, and once the danger of frost has passed, plant out. Place in the sunniest spot in your garden. Space plants 45cm (18in) apart.

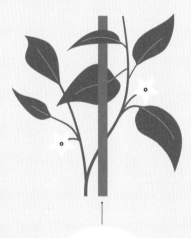

Large varieties may need supporting with a small cane to stop them falling over

⊕ Know how – Pollinating indoor-grown chillies

If you choose to grow plants indoors, open windows to allow pollinators access to the flowers. Or pollinate them yourself, by dabbing the centre of each flower with a paint brush.

Harvest

Use a knife or secateurs to cut fruit from the stem. If grown under cover, the first fruits will be ready to pick in July, and from August if grown outdoors, but before the first frost.

The more mature the fruit, the more colourful and better flavoured it will be. But if you pick fruit when it is green, you will encourage a larger crop. If left, the fruit will shrivel and dry on the plant. You can harvest this and use as cooking flakes.

Eat

Varieties such as *pubescens* can be eaten fresh, in salsas or stuffed with cheese, pork or beef. While *chinense* varieties can be used to marinade meat.

Store

Dried chilli peppers last a long time. Chop chillies in half, remove seeds and spread out on a baking tray. Place in an oven at 150°C (300°F/Gas 2) for eight hours. Leave door slightly ajar and check regularly to ensure the chillies don't burn. Cool, then store in sealed jars.

Tomatoes

Solanum lycopersicum

SEEDS

Storage: up to 4 years
Germination: 7–12 days

POT STARS

Most tomatoes will grow
happily in large pots.
Try 'Tumbler' in a
hanging basket

GOOD COMPANIONS

Grow near chives, mint
and French marigolds.
Basil improves flavour and
deters aphids

Not strictly vegetables but fruits, tomatoes belong to the nightshade family, which includes peppers, potatoes and aubergines.

Homegrown tomatoes are a pleasure and there's a world of cultivars to try. Choose one that best suits your space – patio, hanging basket or balcony – and grow it from seed. Tomatoes need a warm, sheltered spot, and high light intensity, so if you don't have a greenhouse, opt for an indoor variety.

Sow seeds in the spring. Keep them watered, fed and warm, then you will enjoy a glut of juicy fruits all summer. The hardest part is choosing which variety to grow.

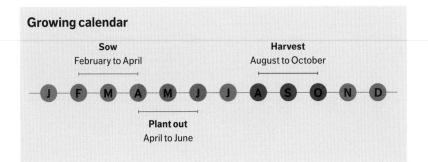

Growing calendar

Sow
February to April

Harvest
August to October

J F M A M J J A S O N D

Plant out
April to June

Varieties

The wild form of tomato originated in the Andes, but its descendants still hanker for a mountainous climate: being frost-tender, and intolerant of extremely hot or dry weather.

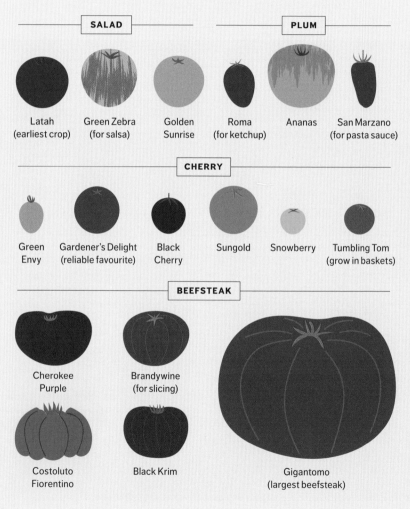

SALAD

Latah
(earliest crop)

Green Zebra
(for salsa)

Golden
Sunrise

PLUM

Roma
(for ketchup)

Ananas

San Marzano
(for pasta sauce)

CHERRY

Green
Envy

Gardener's Delight
(reliable favourite)

Black
Cherry

Sungold

Snowberry

Tumbling Tom
(grow in baskets)

BEEFSTEAK

Cherokee
Purple

Brandywine
(for slicing)

Costoluto
Fiorentino

Black Krim

Gigantomo
(largest beefsteak)

BUSH
Known as 'determinate' tomatoes; grows vertically, then forms sideshoots; doesn't need heavy pruning; suitable for outdoor containers; try 'Rutgers', 'Roma' and 'Celebrity'. Fruit ripens all at once

VINE
Known as indeterminate, cordon, vining or single-stem; grows tall; requires removal of suckers and staking or they fall over; try 'Beefstake', 'Goldie' and 'Cherry'. Produces and ripens fruit through the season

Sow

Start off in pots
Sow one or two seeds in 9cm (3½in) pots filled with compost. Place on a sunny windowsill. Pop a plastic bag over the top, held in place with an elastic band. When the seedlings emerge after a couple of weeks, keep them warm and keep the soil moist. Continue to grow indoors for around eight weeks.

Start off in module trays
If you have space outdoors to grow lots of plants, start the seeds off in a tray. Fill each cell with compost, pop the seed in, add a little more soil and then a little water. Firm well to provide a supportive root zone.

After four weeks, transfer seedlings into 9cm (3½in) pots, discarding any weak seedlings. Move to a sunny windowsill to grow on for another four weeks.

Grow

Plant out into growbags or pots
Harden off. Plant out in growbags or 30cm (12in) pots when all risk of frost has passed, the plants are 15–20cm (6–8in) tall and the flowers of the first truss are beginning to open. Place no more than two plants in each growbag or one in each pot.

They need a sunny, sheltered spot – such as a south-facing wall or balcony – as frost, cold winds and draughts may kill them. Water little and often.

Plant out in a raised bed or border
Prepare the soil by digging in compost or well-rotted manure and apply an organic compound fertilizer, such as fish, blood and bone. Plant vine tomatoes 30cm (12in) apart and bush tomatoes 60cm (2ft) apart.

→ Know how – Training vine tomatoes

SUPPORT STEM
Tie the central stem to a cane for support as the plant grows. Tie the knot on the cane, not on the plant

PINCH OUT
'Pinch out' (remove) shoots at the joint where the leaf stems grow from the main stem

REMOVE TRUSSES
Take off lower 'trusses' (branches) to let light and air reach the fruits

TOPPING
Snip off the top of the central stem in late summer so existing fruit can develop

Aftercare

Container-grown plants need more frequent watering than those in the ground. And in general, tomatoes need a lot of water to produce tasty fruit. Feeding will also encourage fruit development. Once flowers appear, apply an organic, general-purpose feed every 10–14 days. When fruit appears, switch to a high-potassium feed, such as seaweed.

Green tomatoes can be picked, then ripened indoors

Know how – Solving tomato woes

BLIGHT

Caused by warm, wet conditions; presents as brown spots on leaves; remove affected foliage and fruit immediately

BLOSSOM END ROT

Caused by irregular watering, leading to soil drying out; black patches appear at the bottom of the tomato

SPLITTING

Split tomatoes can be a sign of overwatering; keep compost consistently moist

Harvest

For maximum sweetness, stop watering for a couple of days before harvesting. Ripen green tomatoes indoors by putting in a sealed, transparent box.

Store

Keep for several days at room temperature and avoid putting in the fridge. But you can freeze any leftover fruits.

Tomatillos

Physalis philadelphica

SEEDS
Storage: up to 4 years
Germination: 12 days

GROWING CALENDAR
Sow: March to April
Plant out: May
Harvest: August to
October

An essential ingredient for Mexican cuisine, tomatillos give green salsa a sweet, citrus flavour. Also known as the Mexican husk tomato or ground cherry, these small, round, green or purple fruits grow encased in a beautiful papery, lantern-shaped husk.

Tomatillos are not self-pollinating, so for the flowers to set fruit, grow at least two plants. They are prolific. Each plant will produce about 450g (1lb) of fruit – enough for a couple of jars of homemade salsa.

Sow

Start off in pots or module trays
Sow the seeds in small pots or in module trays and place on a warm, sunny windowsill until they germinate. Transplant into 9cm (3½in) pots when the seedlings are 5cm (2in) tall. Keep the soil moist, but not over-wet. Harden the seedlings off (see p.33).

Grow

In May, move the plants outdoors to a warm, sunny, sheltered spot. Plant deeply into the soil, burying around two-thirds of the plant and spacing them at least 60cm (2ft) apart. Alternatively, transfer into large pots filled with potting compost.

Unlike tomatoes, tomatillos don't need to be staked. When they reach 30cm (12in) tall, the main growing stem will flop to the ground. This is normal, and allows the plant to send out new roots. Feed with an organic potash fertilizer, such as wood ash. Keep the soil evenly moist and mulch to suppress weeds.

Harvest

Harvest at the end of summer. Pick when the fruit is still green but has swelled so that the paper lanterns start to split. Store in their husks for up to a week in a paper bag in the fridge. Tomatillos can be frozen if removed from their husks and rinsed and dried before being placed in freezer bags.

Eat

These tart, green fruit are perfect in salsa verde, sauces, soups and guacamoles. Also try them with pork or chicken in soups and sandwiches.

Squash

Pumpkins are actually squash – but a particular type. Squash are either tender summer fruits or hard-skinned winter varieties. The types we all make lanterns from have orange-yellow flowers, bright orange skin and hard, furrowed stems. But there are also pumpkin-squash, which typically have yellow, smooth skin.

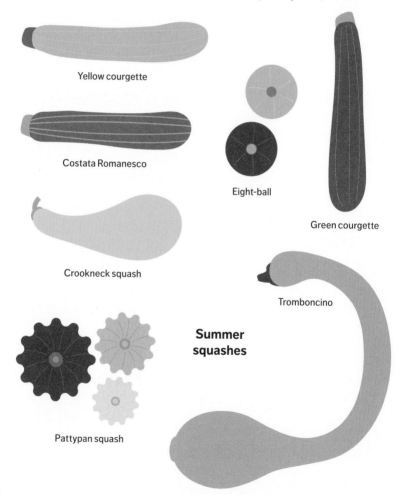

Yellow courgette

Costata Romanesco

Eight-ball

Green courgette

Crookneck squash

Tromboncino

Summer squashes

Pattypan squash

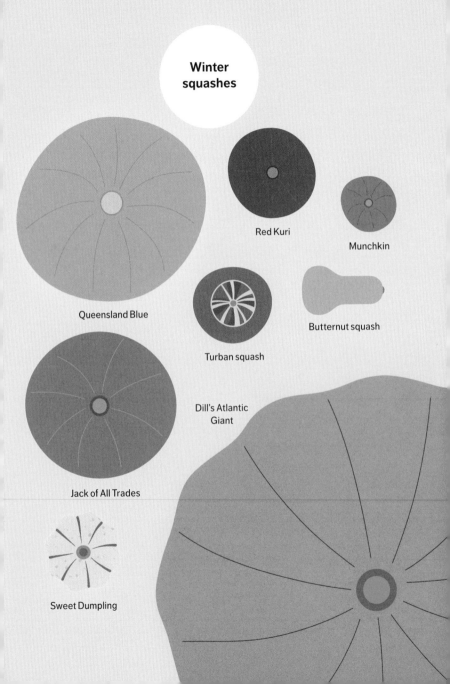

Winter squashes

Red Kuri

Munchkin

Queensland Blue

Butternut squash

Turban squash

Dill's Atlantic Giant

Jack of All Trades

Sweet Dumpling

Courgettes/ Zucchini

Cucurbita pepo

SEEDS
Storage: up to 5 years
Germination: 5–8 days

POT STARS
Try Courgette
'Midnight'

GOOD COMPANIONS
Beans, radish, nasturtiums, marigolds. Calendula flowers will attract the insects that pollinate courgette flowers

Courgettes can be so vigorous and prolific that, if you get them to grow, the biggest problem can be a glut of watery marrows in late summer. Courgettes are simply immature marrows – and because of their firmer texture, many people prefer them to marrows. One solution to gluts (apart from giving away to friends) is to experiment with as many different summer squashes (see p.92) as your space allows.

They are an easy plant to care for. Large leaves reduce the need for weeding and courgettes grow very quickly. The availability of climbing varieties makes these delicious vegetables a possibility for balcony gardeners, too. Courgettes are insect-pollinated but in cold seasons, you could hand-pollinate to ensure that fruit will set. Simply transfer pollen from the stamen of the male flower to the stigma of the female flower.

Growing calendar

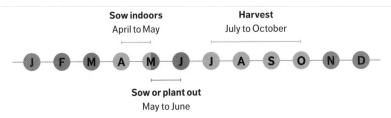

Sow indoors
April to May

Harvest
July to October

J F M A M J J A S O N D

Sow or plant out
May to June

Varieties

The fruits can be solid green, creamy yellow, stripy, long or round. Even the flowers are an edible delicacy. 'Black Forest' is a vertical climber for balconies. Try 'Zephyr' for a nutty flavour and creamy yellow fruits, and 'Shooting Star' for striking yellow fruits that taste fab in salads and stir-fries.

Sow

Start off in pots

Soak seeds in water overnight before sowing. Fill 7.5cm (3in) pots with compost. Sow two seeds vertically, about 2.5cm (1in) deep, and cover with compost. Place a clear plastic bag over the pot and hold it in place with an elastic band. Place the pot on a windowsill. When the seeds germinate, remove the weaker of the two. Harden the plants off before planting out.

Sow directly outdoors (early summer)

Alternatively, in early summer, you can sow seeds directly into the ground. Add plenty of well-rotted manure or compost to the soil beforehand. Plant seeds on their sides and space bush types 90cm (3ft) apart and trailing types 1.2–2m (4–6½ft) apart. Alternatively, sow into a large pot filled with compost.

Grow

For plants that have been started off indoors, plant out no more than two plants per growbag or one plant per pot in early June. Space them at least 60–90cm (2–3ft) apart, depending on the variety (trailing types need more room).

Water regularly during the growing period, around the plants but not over the leaves. When fruits appear, feed every 10–14 days with an organic, high-potassium fertilizer, such as wood ash.

⊙ Know how – Solving courgette woes

Powdery mildew is a fungal infection that affects a plant's productivity. Symptoms include a blotchy white coating on the leaves. To avoid problems, space plants well to ensure good air flow, water regularly during hot weather and mulch around the base of the plant, leaving the soil mulch-free close to the base of the stem.

Harvest

Harvest courgettes regularly through the summer and autumn. Picking encourages further fruit growth. Cut from the stem with a sharp knife.

An unpicked courgette will quickly turn into a marrow

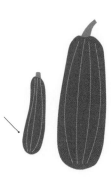

Eat

Female flower   Male flower

Flowers and young shoots
A courgette's delicate flowers and young shoots are also edible. But they are rarely available in shops because they don't last long once picked. Pick the male flowers (with no fruit attached) but leave a few for the bees. Stuff flowers with ricotta, lemon zest and pine nuts, then dip in a beer batter and deep-fry until golden.

Store

Providing it is not bruised, the hard skin of courgettes keeps the flesh inside moist for several weeks. Store courgettes in a cool place away from direct heat and don't drop them. You can chop off slices as and when required.

Pumpkins

Cucurbita pepo, C. moschata, C. maxima

Halloween may make the most of the pumpkin's decorative qualities but it is a very versatile veg and is wonderfully nutritious and delicious. Packed with vitamin A and antioxidants, pumpkins are also recommended for controlling cholesterol.

A fast-growing, creeping vine, pumpkin plants need room to spread as well as a sunny, sheltered spot. Plant seeds after the last spring frost has passed and when the soil is warm enough for seeds to germinate. They can also be grown in growbags or containers.

SEEDS
Storage: up to 5 years
Germination: 5–8 days

POT STARS
'Jack Be Little'

GOOD COMPANIONS
Grow near beans, radish, nasturtium, marigold

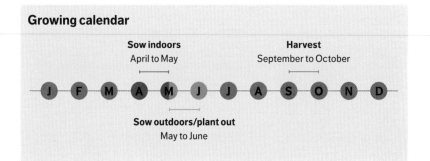

Growing calendar

Sow indoors	Harvest
April to May	September to October

J F M A M J J A S O N D

Sow outdoors/plant out
May to June

Varieties

Pumpkins and pumpkin-squash vary widely in colour, texture, taste and size. There are the record-breaking characters, like 'Dill's Atlantic Giant', but more modest-sized cultivars are also available.

'Jack Be Little' produces mini pumpkins that fit in your palm. 'Munchkin' is another dinky variety that makes a spectacular ornamental climber for arches and frames. 'Rouge Vif d'Etamps' is a stunning pumpkin with red, ribbed skin.

Sow

Start off in pots
Soak seeds overnight, then sow them on their sides at a depth of 2.5cm (1in) in a 9cm (3½in) pot. Place pots inside a plastic bag and position in a warm, bright spot. Once a few leaves have appeared, move to a cooler spot. When risk of frost has passed, harden off. Plant outside in early June in a sunny, moisture-retentive soil, sheltered from cold wind.

Sow directly outdoors
Prepare planting pockets two weeks before sowing seed. Make a hole about one spade's depth, width and height, and fill with compost and well-rotted manure and soil. Sow seeds at least 1m (40in) apart from May to June (distances vary so check specific cultivar requirements).

Grow

It takes around 120 days for most types of pumpkin to grow from seed, although giant cultivars need up to 150 days. Water at the base of plants in very dry weather, avoiding the leaves to prevent powdery mildew. Feed every two weeks with wood ash once fruits start to swell. Don't let the fruits sit on the wet ground as they may rot. Instead, place them on an upturned seed tray or tile on the surface of the soil. Cut the top off the main shoot to divert energy into the fruit.

Harvest

Pick pumpkins before the first frost. Cut away leaves in early autumn, exposing the skin of the fruit. This will help them to fully ripen.

When fruits start to change colour, gradually reduce the watering. This will increase the fruit's storage life.

Once a pumpkin is ripe, cut it away from the plant, leaving as much of the stalk attached to the pumpkin as possible. Leave in the sun for 10 days. This 'curing' process will harden its skin. But cover at night if frost is forecast.

Train shoots in circles on the ground to prevent long stems from spreading too far

Eat

LEAVES: Cut the tips and young leaves off trailing stems once three or four fruits have formed. These tender greens are edible and can be steamed, fried or simmered.

FLOWERS: As with courgette flowers, pumpkin flowers can be eaten. But pick only the males. These are identifiable by their long, wiry stems (female flowers have shorter, thicker stalks).

SEEDS: Rinse, spread over a baking sheet, season and drizzle with olive oil. Bake for 10 minutes in the oven at 150°C (300°F/Gas 2). Let them cool, then store in a jar.

Store

Once cured, leave indoors in a cool, well-ventilated spot. A slatted shelf or net is ideal. Stored this way, winter squashes will keep for months.

Cucumbers

Cucumis sativus

SEEDS
Storage: up to 5 years
Germination: 5–8 days

POT STARS
'La Diva' produces mini
fruit that will grow well in
a container

GOOD COMPANIONS
Grow near dill, sweetcorn,
radishes, sunflowers.
Avoid potatoes and
aromatic herbs

This annual climber is an essential summer crop, whose crisp, juicy texture is a must for salads.

You can grow this creeping vine in the ground or in containers, and some can be grown in a greenhouse. To yield the best quality fruit, you need to avoid cool or shaded locations and should provide plenty of moisture and nutrients.

But remember, if you opt for an indoor spot, you must plant an indoor variety. Indoor-grown cucumbers are known as 'parthenocarpic', meaning that the fruit develops without seeds and without pollination. Outdoors, you have more choice of varieties, and bees are free to visit your plants (they can cause deformity in parthenocarpic varieties).

Growing calendar

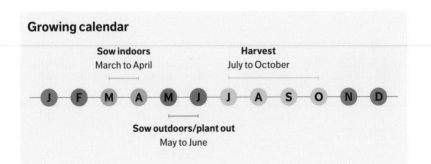

Sow indoors
March to April

Harvest
July to October

J F M A M J J A S O N D

Sow outdoors/plant out
May to June

Varieties

'Femdan' is a dark fruit for indoor plots, as is the cultivar 'Zeina', which produces short fruits. 'Marketmore' produces a ridged fruit with a trailing habit that thrives outside. Other fun varieties to try are 'Lemon', which has tennis ball-sized, yellow fruit, or 'Northern Pickling', an early variety that is great for salads and pickling.

CUCUMBER TYPES

RIDGE
Outdoor varieties; stubby fruit with rough skin; try 'Burpless Tasty Green' and 'Green Fingers'

JAPANESE
Long, slender smooth-skinned fruit; usually requires training up a pole or net; try 'Tokiwa' and 'Sooyow Nishiki'

PICKLING
Short and stout varieties, with dry flesh for pickling or eating fresh. Stores well. Try 'Vorgebirgstrauben'

Sow

Start off in pots
Sow the seed on their sides 1cm (½in) deep in 7.5cm (3in) pots filled with compost. Pop a plastic bag over the pot, held in place with an elastic band. Germination takes around two weeks, at which point move to a bright, sunny windowsill. Keep compost moist, not wet. Harden off before planting out.

Sow directly outdoors
Sow three seeds of an outdoor variety in May or June, on their sides and 1cm (½in) deep into rich soil at a distance of 90cm (3ft) apart. Thin out to leave the strongest seedling.

Grow

Move plants started off in pots to a sunny, sheltered position in early June. Plant into a hole filled with garden compost or well-rotted manure. Space the plants 30–60cm (12–24in) apart, depending on the variety. Protect with fleece or cloches. Plenty of water around the base of the plants is essential. Keep soil moist and ensure there's no drought stress during flowering and fruiting.

Pinch out the plant's growing tip and the tips of flowerless sideshoots once seven leaves have developed. When the fruits appear, apply an organic, high potash feed, such as wood ash every couple of weeks. Cucumber vines can be left to scramble over the ground or can be trained to climb up poles or netting.

⊕ Know how – Cucumber pollination

Outdoors, insects will pollinate the yellow flowers but this requires both male and female flowers, so don't remove any. But do remove male flowers from greenhouse cucumbers. Male flowers are identifiable by their plain stalk (female flowers have a swollen bulge between the bottom of the flower and the stem).

Harvest

Cut from the stem with a sharp knife when the fruits are around 15cm (6in), or around 10cm (4in) for pickling types. Harvest young for best taste – don't wait for huge cucumbers to develop. Regular harvesting encourages more growth.

Cucamelons

Melothria scabra

These miniature watermelons are fun and productive, and will bring a touch of the exotic to your garden. Grape-size cucamelon fruits, which hail from Central America, taste like cucumbers with a dash of lime. But they are easier to grow than cucumbers and are fairly pest-free to boot.

These highly productive vines are happy in pots, in hanging baskets or on a warm, bright windowsill. They will also thrive in the UK climate. Other names are Mexican sour gherkins and mouse melons.

SEEDS
Storage: up to 5 years
Germination: 2–4 weeks

POT STARS
Plant one plant per
20cm (8in) container

GROWING CALENDAR
Sow: April to May indoors
Harvest: July to September

Sow

Start off in a seed tray
Scatter five or six seeds in a tray. Give each seed plenty of space and push the blunt end downwards into the compost just out of sight. Water. Ensure the seeds get plenty of heat to help them germinate. They need a temperature of around 24°C (75°F), so place on a sunny windowsill. Seeds should take around four weeks to germinate.

Grow

When plants reach 5–7.5cm (2–3in) tall, pot on into 7.5cm (3in) pots. Then, when tendrils begin to grow, replant into 20cm (8in) pots. Plants can stay in these pots and can be placed outdoors in a sheltered spot, once hardened off and all risk of frost has past.

Give the trailing vines some support to climb up – wire or a frame of pea sticks work well. Keep compost moist and water around the plant, not on the foliage. Use an organic, high-potash feed. Pinch out the tops once plants are well established.

Harvest

Pick from mid-summer onwards when the fruits are grape-sized and firm.

Eat

SALADS AND SALSAS: Pick off the vine and add to a salad or serve as a side dish mixed with olive oil and salt. You can also use them in salsas.

COCKTAILS: Serve them in drinks at a cocktail party as a stylish homegrown garnish.

PICKLE: Pickle in white wine vinegar in a jar with mint and dill.

Sweetcorn/Corn

Zea mays

SEEDS
Storage: up to 2 years
Germination: 10–12 days

POT STARS
'Strawberry Popcorn'

GOOD COMPANIONS
Grow near peas, beans,
squash, cucumber,
sunflowers, parsley

A fast-growing annual, sweetcorn is cultivated across the globe for its delicious, edible, golden-yellow kernels.

This frost-tender vegetable must start life under glass. Once outside, its female flowers – known as silks – will ensure fertilization by catching pollen on the wind.

Sweetcorn – which is a type of grass – is typically grown on garden plots or allotments, where it is grown in blocks. It will only yield a small number of cobs – sometimes only one or two – from each plant. However, mini sweetcorn is well suited to smaller gardens and even to containers.

Once established, sweetcorn is surprisingly easy to grow. Make sure it's planted in a sheltered spot away from strong winds, and in rich, well-draining soil.

Growing calendar

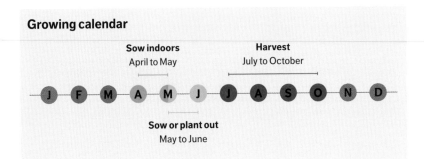

Sow indoors
April to May

Harvest
July to October

J F M A M J J A S O N D

Sow or plant out
May to June

Sow

Start off in pots

Prepare the plot where your sweetcorn will eventually be planted by spreading it with a layer of well-rotted manure.

Soak the seeds overnight before sowing. Sow one or two seeds per 7.5cm (3in) pot, 2.5cm (1in) deep. Coir jiffy pots are ideal as they can be planted straight into the ground, which means the sweetcorn's sensitive roots won't be disturbed when they're transplanted. Water and place on a sunny windowsill or in a cold frame.

Feed after three weeks with an organic, general-purpose fertilizer. When the seedlings have three or four leaves, harden them off.

Grow

When all risk of frost has passed, plant the seedlings in a sheltered, sunny spot. Space them 2.5cm (1in) deep and 40cm (16in) apart and be sure to plant them in blocks to aid pollination by wind.

Mulch to conserve moisture and stake tall plants.

Cover any roots that appear with a mulch of compost or grass clippings.

When plants are 15cm (6in) tall, feed with an organic fertilizer, such as blood meal. Water in dry conditions, when flowering starts and when the grains begin to swell.

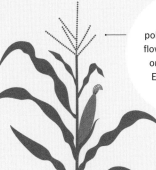

Wind-blown pollen from the male flowers (tassels) falls on the silks below. Each silk leads to a kernel

Tap the plant top when male flower 'tassels' open; this helps pollinate the female silks below.

Female silks are sticky to catch pollen, then shrivel as corn ears mature

Harvest

You can tell when the cobs are ripe for picking by doing a bit of investigation. Once the female silks turn brown, carefully pull back the sheath and press a kernel with your fingernail. If it exudes a creamy liquid, your corn is ready. But if it is watery, it isn't yet ripe, and if it is paste-like, it is past its best.

Eat & store

Freshness matters. Once cobs are picked, the sugar converts to starch and the cobs lose their sweetness. Cooking quickly after picking preserves the flavour. If you are keeping them for more than a day, parboil for one minute and place in the fridge wrapped in clingfilm. Try turning parboiled cobs into fritters, stew or soup.

Podded vegetables

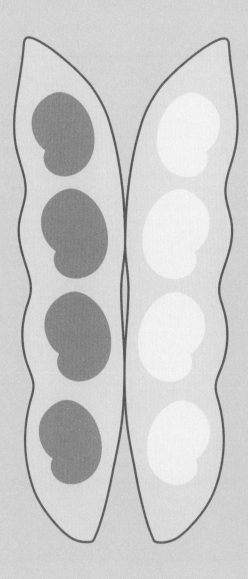

SEEDS
Storage: up to 3 years
Germination: 7–14 days

POT STARS
Try 'The Sutton' in
containers

GOOD COMPANIONS
Grow near summer savory,
potatoes, sweetcorn

½ actual size

Broad beans/ Fava beans

Vicia faba

Hailing from the legume family, broad beans – or fava beans, horse beans and tick beans, as they are also known – are a high-protein food that are edible both as seeds and as young pods.

Broad beans are a fantastic pick-me-up, stimulating the brain to produce dopamine, the chemical associated with happiness.

And they cheer up your soil, too. Sow them as a green manure crop (see p.38) and they will create a nitrogen-rich soil that is the basis for healthy, strong plants. Simply cut the stem to the ground after harvesting and leave the roots in place.

While the leathery pods of the broad beans generally all look the same, the beans that grow inside can be round or kidney-shaped, white, green or red.

Growing calendar

Sow
March to May

J F M A M J J A S O N D

Harvest
June to September

LONGPOD
Long and narrow pods with 8–10 kidney-shaped beans. 'Imperial Green'

WINDSOR
Shorter and broader than longpods, with 4–7 beans in each pod. 'Green Windsor'

DWARF
Plants produce short pods and only reach around 40cm (16in) tall. Suited to containers. 'Bonny Lad'

Sow

Sow directly outdoors
Choose a well-drained, sheltered site and improve the soil with garden compost or well-rotted manure before sowing. Sow your seeds 4cm (1½in) deep, 22.5cm (9in) apart, and in rows 22.5cm (9in) apart. But check the instructions on the seed packet as planting distances can vary according to the cultivar.

Grow

Give the plants a good soaking when flowers begin to appear, unless there has been a lot of rain. Increase the watering when the pods appear. Hoe regularly to keep the weeds in check. Tall cultivars may need staking.

⊕ Know how – Dealing with blackfly

Pinch off the growing tips of the stem when the first beans start to form to protect plants from the blackfly aphid, which likes the growing tips best. This pest can be kept at bay by encouraging natural predators – such as hoverflies and ladybirds – to your garden. If beans do get infested, squash insects with your fingers.

Harvest

Bigger isn't necessarily better when it comes to beans – smaller beans have better flavour. Pick some when the pods are 5–7.5cm (2–3in) long and cook them whole. Pick beans for shelling when the beans begin to show through the pod and the scar on the shelled beans is white or green (not black).

When dug into the soil after harvest, this plant will nourish the soil for the next crop

Cut the beans off the plant with a knife or secateurs. Once cropping has finished, leave plants on your plot as a green manure – just cut them down, leaving the roots intact.

Eat

Freshness is crucial to taste. Young leaves are edible and very nutritious. They can be cooked and have a spinach-like flavour.

Store

Beans will keep in their pods for three days, longer in the fridge. Blanch shelled beans and freeze.

SEEDS
Storage: up to 3 years
Germination: 7–14 days

POT STARS
Climbing beans can be
trained up a tepee of
canes in a large pot

GOOD COMPANIONS
Nasturtiums.
Avoid ground that's
recently had beans
growing on it

French beans/ Green beans

Phaseolus vulgaris

A member of the *Leguminosae* family, French beans, common beans or green beans, as they are also known, are a frost-tender annual that will produce a reliable crop in most climates. Since they are self-fertile plants, they flower and form beans with ease, providing a generous crop come harvest time.

Like broad beans, French beans can also be grown as a green manure to suppress weeds, add fertility and control soil erosion (see p.38).

Varieties
French beans come in climbing (pole) varieties and dwarf (bush) bean varieties. Pods vary in size, and can be round or flat. 'Dutch Brown' is a dwarf variety for drying, while 'Chevrier Vert' is grown for flageolets.

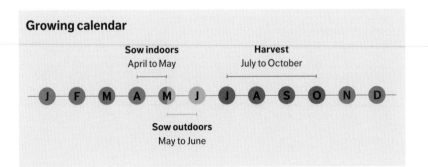

Growing calendar

Sow indoors
April to May

Harvest
July to October

J F M A M J J A S O N D

Sow outdoors
May to June

Sow

Start off in seed or module trays
Pre-germinate French bean seeds (see opposite). Sow in seed trays or module trays and keep in a sunny spot. Harden off. Plant the seedlings out when they are 5cm (2in) tall and all risk of frost has passed.

Sow directly outdoors
Choose a sunny, sheltered site, with fertile, well-draining soil. Apply a general organic feed two weeks before planting. If sowing in April, warm the ground with cloches or wait until May.

Sow dwarf seeds 5cm (2in) deep, 20cm (8in) apart and in rows 60cm (2ft) apart. For climbing varieties, sow two seeds per station at 5cm (2in) deep, 25cm (10in) apart and in rows 60cm (2ft) apart. Alternatively, grow them onto a tepee structure (see p.123). Two outdoor sowings, three weeks apart, will ensure a long harvest.

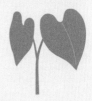

Grow

Protect seedlings from slugs and hoe to keep weeds at bay. Mulch around the stems with well-rotted manure and don't let the soil dry out, particularly when flowers are forming. Support dwarf varieties with pea sticks; climbing varieties need sturdy canes (see pp.122–123).

Slugs and blackfly can be a problem, as is red spider mite during hot summers (see p.195).

Harvest

Beans are ready to harvest in 7–12 weeks.
Ready-to-pick pods should snap off easily. Keep
on picking to encourage further yields. Feed the
plants after harvesting.

Pods can be
yellow, flecked,
red or purple, as
well as green

⊘ Know how – Pre-germinating French beans

Spread seeds on a piece of damp kitchen roll. Keep moist. When shoots begin
to appear, sow seeds in pots or outside. Discard beans that don't plump up.

Eat

You can eat beans and pods whole. But you can grow varieties, such as
flageolets, that are picked before full maturity and taste particularly good
fresh. Haricot bean varieties, which have white seeds, are brilliant for
absorbing flavours of soups or stews. Cook soon after harvesting. The whole
pod is edible. Pair with potatoes and cook into a curry. French beans also
make great chutney.

Store

Wash, trim, slice, blanch and freeze. They will keep, frozen, for a few months.

Supports for climbers

Climbing beans and peas need support. While seedlings start off small, they flourish into strapping vines laden with leaves and pods. Whichever support structure you choose to adopt, ensure it is sturdy enough for the plant to clamber up and that it can withstand winds.

Why support plants?

Support structures encourage heavier cropping and make veg easier to harvest. They also allow air and light to reach the plant. By growing crops vertically, the gardener is also able to conserve space.

Climbing plants can be grown up tepees made from a range of materials; bamboo canes, which are straight and long-lasting, or coppiced wood such as hazel, dogwood or willow – which are more sustainable options. Peas and beans need their support structure once they have put out their first tendrils – spiral threads that enable them to cling and pull themselves aloft. Plant up to two plants either side of each cane.

A three sisters garden

This is a native American method of growing sweetcorn, squash and beans together in a 'sisterly' support system designed to help each plant thrive. In this arrangement, sweetcorn offer beans a living trellis to climb, beans keep the soil fertile and squash leaves work as a living mulch that prevents weeds from germinating and locks in soil moisture.

How to tie

Take care when tying your plant to its support: tying string too tightly around the stem can rub and wound it. To avoid this, secure string tightly around a stake but loosely around the plant. Following this principle, create a figure of eight loop between the stem and stake. This will provide support while also allowing the plant to move.

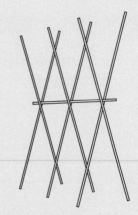

A simple tepee: This structure is ideal for a small plot. Make using three 2.5m (8ft) canes tied together with string at the top.

A large tepee: Place canes 2.5m (8ft) in a conical shape, 15cm (6in) apart, and tie securely at the top with string.

Bike wheel trellis: Create using two bicycle wheels. Tie strings to holes where the spokes used to be, make taught and peg to the ground. Support using a central pole.

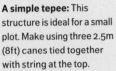

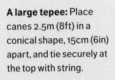

Double row: Make two rows using 2.5m (8ft) canes crossed at the top and secured to a horizontal bar. Space rows 50cm (20in) apart, and lay canes 15cm (6in) apart along the row.

The 'X': Cross pairs of 2.5m (8ft) canes and hold together with a horizontal cane. Secure the binding points. This frame gives plants more air and space. It also makes it easier to see – and pick – the beans.

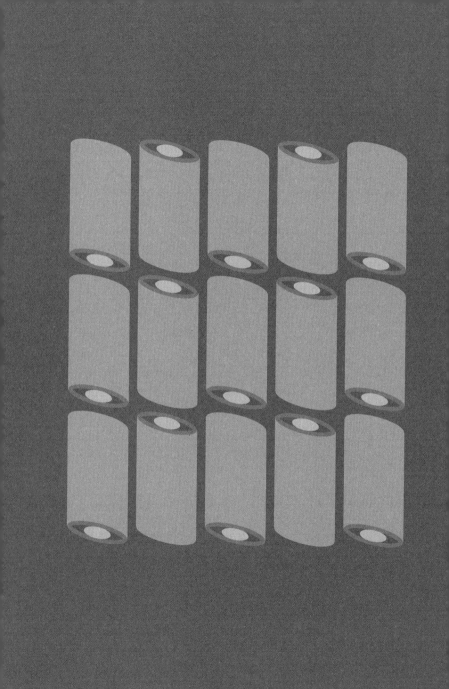

SEEDS
Storage: up to 3 years
Germination: 7–14 days

POT STARS
Dwarf runner beans don't
need much space

GOOD COMPANIONS
Grow near celeriac,
cauliflowers and sweet
peas. Grow away from
onion and fennel

Runner beans/ String beans

Phaseolus coccineus

Commonly known as runner beans or scarlet runner beans, these climbing plants are grown for their edible pods and seeds.

This frost-tender plant will scramble up poles, netting and strings. A generous plant, it will reward gardeners with bumper harvests, and it also has pretty, nectar-rich flowers for bees and butterflies.

Prepare ground early on, leaving plenty of space to set up cane supports later. Runner beans can be grown in pots, too. But use large containers that allow room for a cane tepee (see p.123). Alternatively, grow a dwarf variety that doesn't need supporting. You'll be busy watering all summer; beans need plenty of moisture when flowers appear. And once pods are ready, your main duty will be keeping on top of harvesting.

Growing calendar

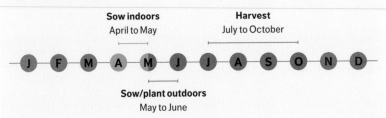

Sow indoors
April to May

Harvest
July to October

J F M A M J J A S O N D

Sow/plant outdoors
May to June

Varieties

'Polestar' is tasty and tender, and freezes well. 'Enorma' produces huge pods. 'Achievement' is a heavy-yielding, red-flowered variety. 'Mergoles' has white flowers, while 'Sunset' has salmon-pink flowers. Or try dwarf runner bean plants such as 'Hestia', an attractive bushy variety, and 'Hammond's Dwarf Scarlet'.

Sow

Start off in pots

Prepare your site in the autumn, digging in some well-rotted manure, straw or compost – runner beans don't like poor soils.

Start seeds indoors in small pots, planting them around 5cm (2in) deep. They take around 10 days to germinate. When all risk of frost has passed, and when they are well established in their pots, harden off and plant outside. Sow climbers in double rows, spacing rows 50cm (20in) apart, and canes 15cm (6in) apart along the row. Or grow in circles around a tepee of canes (see p.123).

Sow directly outdoors

Before sowing, make a tepee support (see p.123) for climbing beans. Sow two seeds to each cane support, 5cm (2in) deep and with a 15cm (6in) gap between plants. Or plant against a wall, and allow them to climb up a net.

Grow

Thin out the weaker of the two seedlings and protect from the usual predators, especially slugs. Loosely tie the young plants to the canes. Runners will wend their way naturally around any supports, so there's no need to tie plants in once they've started to wrap themselves around their canes.

Apply mulch after planting out, to keep soil moist. Beans need regular watering, especially once the plant has flowers and pods. Flowers will appear about four weeks after sowing seed. To encourage pollination, attract insects by growing sweet peas with the beans.

Harvest

Pinch out the top of the plants when they reach the top of the cane. Beans will be ready around 60 days after sowing seed.

Harvest once the pods are 20cm (8in) long – the older they get, the tougher they become. Pick frequently to encourage the plant to produce new beans, which it will for up to three months. Once all the beans have been harvested, dig the roots into the soil to improve soil fertility (see pp.38–39).

Young pods are best but if you've left beans too long, discard the pods and use mature beans inside for cooking

Eat & store

Runner beans are prolific. They will keep for up to five days in the fridge but gluts can be frozen. Slice, blanch and store in the freezer for 3–6 months. Or give away to friends!

Alternatively, you can dry your glut of beans. Pod them and dry the beans in a warm, airy place, then store in an airtight container. Then use them as you would other dried beans – in soups and stews.

Peas

Pisum sativum

SEEDS
Storage: up to 2 years
Germination: 7–10 days

POT STARS
'Bingo' is a short variety,
perfect for containers

GOOD COMPANIONS
Plant near turnip, garlic,
radish

With their sweet, juicy seeds and crisp, crunchy pods, peas are one of the most rewarding veg of the summer season. In fact, pea plants provide three veg in one: mangetout (also known as snow peas, picked when the pods are just beginning to swell), sugar snaps (picked a little later) and regular peas (picked even later, once the pods have become inedible).

Peas are also worth growing for their delicate, butterfly-like blooms in shades of lavender, pink, purple and blue.

Growing peas requires diligence over moisture levels. The soil needs water to help pods swell, so check in with your pea bed regularly and apply a layer of mulch around the base of the plants.

Plants can climb up to 3m (10ft) tall, but shorter varieties are available for pot-grown peas.

Growing calendar

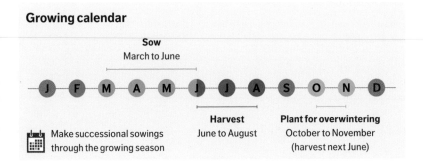

Sow
March to June

J F M A M J J A S O N D

Harvest
June to August

Plant for overwintering
October to November
(harvest next June)

Make successional sowings through the growing season

129

MANGETOUT
Flat pods that can
be eaten whole, as
the name suggests;
harvest pods when
7.5cm (3in) long

SUGAR SNAP
Rounded, edible
pods that taste
great raw; harvest
when semi-mature

SHELLING PEAS
Only the peas are
eaten; compost the
pods; varieties are
early or maincrop,
'wrinkled-seed' or
'smooth-seed'

Sow

Sow in pots

Select a dwarf or bush variety such as 'Bingo' or 'Avola'.
Fill a container that is 45cm (18in) across with compost to
about 5cm (2in) below the rim, then insert supports for your
plants to climb. Plant one seed at each support, 2.5cm (1in)
below the soil surface. Cover and water thoroughly. Protect
with cloches to aid germination. When 10–12cm (4–5in) tall,
remove cloches and keep pots in an open, sunny site.

Sow directly outdoors

Prepare soil a few weeks in advance by digging in some well-
rotted compost, which will give peas the rich soil they crave.

While peas dislike high summer temperatures, their seeds
dislike overly wet or cold soil. If the soil isn't warm enough,
wait a while and add a cloche to heat up the bed.

Sow in rows on a warm, dry day from March to June. Make the
drills 15cm (6in) wide and 60–90cm (2–3ft) apart. Plant the
seeds 2.5cm (1in) deep and 5cm (2in) apart. Gently firm the
soil after sowing. Cover with netting to protect from birds.

Grow

Once tendrils have developed, insert pea sticks into the soil for support and to lift the plants off the ground and away from slugs. Position the sticks next to the stems.

Give 2.5cm (1in) of water each week to ensure good growth and be sure to water once a week when flowers appear. When plants are 15cm (6in) tall, add a layer of mulch to keep the weeds down. If the soil is rich, don't add fertilizer – over-feeding can stimulate a lot of leaf growth and divert the plant's energy away from pod production.

Harvest

Pick the pods, working upwards from the base of the plant. Be careful not to uproot the plant; hold the stem with one hand as you go. Cut the stem and leaves for the compost heap but keep the roots in the ground. *Pisum sativum* plants add nitrogen to your soil, which benefits the next crop you grow in that spot (see pp.38–39).

Pick often to encourage new pods

Eat

FLOWERS: Vegetable pea flowers are edible. They are slightly sweet and taste like peas. The shoots and vine tendrils are edible, too, but sweet pea flowers (*Lathyrus odoratus*) are toxic and only grown for ornamental qualities.

Store

Once picked, the sugar in peas turns to starch and their flavour diminishes. Cook or freeze within a few hours of harvesting.

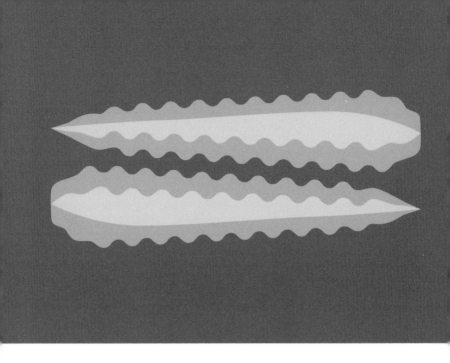

Asparagus peas

Tetragonolobus purpureus

SEEDS
Storage: up to 2 years
Germination: 7–14 days

GROWING CALENDAR
Sow: April to May
Harvest: July to August

Also known as winged pea, winged bean and four-angled bean, owing to the frills that edge the plant's edible pods, these small, shrubby plants produce pods with the taste of asparagus, but they require less room in your border. With trailing branches and luscious maroon flowers, these veg are also comfortable in pots, hanging baskets and under fruit trees. Easy to cultivate, asparagus pea plants are content to flourish in average soil and moisture, and with some sun. They double as attractive ground cover.

Sow

Start off in pots or module trays
In early spring, sow in 7.5cm (3in) pots or modules filled with seed compost. Place on a sunny windowsill until the seeds germinate. Harden off before planting out.

Grow

When all risk of frost has passed, plant seedlings out in fertile, well-raked, well-drained ground in a sunny spot. Sow 10cm (4in) apart, in rows 20–30cm (8–12in) apart.

This scrambling plant will need pea sticks for support, to keep the plants away from slugs and to encourage air circulation. Water in dry weather and increase after flowering. Keep weed-free.

Harvest

Harvest pods regularly and while they are small and tender – no more than 2cm (¾in) long. Older, mature pods are tough and fibrous. Cut plants down to the soil after harvesting for use as a green manure (see pp.38–39).

Eat

Top and tail pods and steam or lightly boil. Slice finely, steam and add to salads and stir-fries or mix with peas into rice dishes. Can also be pickled or coated in tempura batter and fried.

Store

To keep the seeds, let the pods die, dry them, remove the seeds and store the seeds in an airtight container away from direct light.

Bulb & stem vegetables

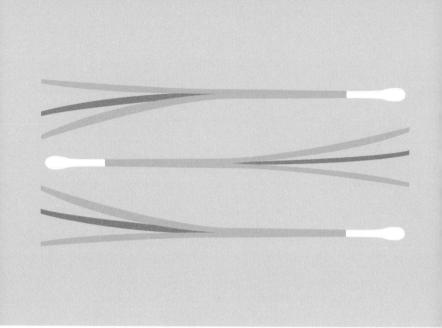

SEEDS
Storage: up to 3 years
Germination: 7–12 days

GROWING CALENDAR
Sow: March to September,
planting new seeds every
three to four weeks for
a continual harvest

GOOD COMPANIONS
Sow among carrots as the
smell deters onion fly. Don't
plant near peas and beans

Spring onions/ Scallions

Allium cepa, A. fistulosum

A quick-growing plant in any fertile soil, spring
onions grow in the very smallest of spaces – even
in the gaps between slow-growing crops.

Some varieties grow a small bulb (*Allium cepa*), while
others have long, straight bulbs (*Allium fistulosum*).

Sow in a well-drained soil little and often to produce
a regular crop from summer to autumn. They are
ready for harvest after eight weeks.

Sow

Sow directly outdoors
Improve the soil in the autumn with well-rotted manure, and rake the soil over. Make shallow drills and sprinkle seeds around 2.5cm (1in) apart. Leave a 10cm (4in) gap between rows.

Sow in pots
Scatter seeds in 20cm (8in) pots, leaving a space of 2cm (¾in) between them. Cover with a 1cm (½in) layer of compost. Keep the surface moist. Place in a sunny spot.

⊖ Know how – Re-growing spring onions
Treat spring onions as a cut-and-come-again vegetable. Simply snip off the stems above the root end and place in a glass of water. The stems will re-grow after a few days.

Grow

When seedlings are around 4cm (1½in) tall, thin out to give plants 2.5–5cm (1–2in) space in each direction. Give a little water if the soil is dry. Hoe away any weeds.

Harvest

Lift the plants when they are small and young, and when they're as thick as a pencil. If they get much thicker, they lose their sweetness. Water plants that remain in the ground.

Eat

Grill on a BBQ with a little olive oil. The leaves can also be grilled or stir-fried. They taste great in a stir-fry paired with garlic and ginger.

Leeks

Allium porrum

SEEDS
Storage: up to 2 years
Germination: 12–16 days

GOOD COMPANIONS
The smell of carrot will deter leek moth from leeks, while leeks deter carrot root fly

This vitamin-rich vegetable is hardy enough to survive the coldest of winters. In fact, it is at its most flavoursome during colder months.

Fairly pest and disease-resistant, leeks are easy to grow but they do require effort and time to get established.

Sow seeds in early spring since they need fairly cool temperatures to germinate. After that, they need full sun and rich, well-drained soil.

As they grow, keep the soil mounded around their stems; this helps produce longer, whiter stems.

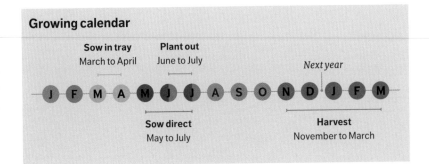

Growing calendar

Sow in tray March to April

Plant out June to July

Next year

J F M A M J J A S O N D J F M

Sow direct May to July

Harvest November to March

Varieties

For thick, flavourful stems, try 'Giant Musselburgh' or 'Carentan'. 'Giant Winter' produces excellent, fine, long white stems that don't mind being left in the ground.

Sow

Sow directly outdoors

Prepare the leek bed in autumn by digging in some well-rotted manure or garden compost. Ensure the bed is lightly firmed but soft underneath. Create rows 30cm (12in) apart.

Sow directly outdoors between March and April. Sow in the rows, about 1cm (½in) deep. Cover with a layer of compost and water. When the seedlings have a few leaves, thin them out, leaving 15cm (6in) between each plant.

Grow

Cover with nets to protect from pests. Hoe weeds and keep well watered in hot weather. To avoid plant stress during dry spells, feed occasionally with liquid seaweed.

⊖ Know how – Blanching

To increase the white (edible) portion of the leek, blanch the plants in stages from August. To do this, draw up 5cm (2in) of dry soil around the stems each time, avoiding the plant leaves.

Harvest

Between mid-autumn to late spring, gently ease the leeks out of the ground by loosening the surrounding soil with a fork. Don't pull the plant straight out of the ground as the stem may snap. Leeks can remain in the ground for as long as you need them through the winter, so don't rush to dig them all up in one go.

Water well while leeks are getting established, but only in dry conditions thereafter

(→) Know how – Leek woes

Look out for leek rust, which presents on leaves as raised orange spots or pustules. To avoid it, keep leaves dry and use rust-resistant varieties.

Leeks can 'bolt', which results in the appearance of flower stems and the halting of vegetable growth. Planting seeds at the right time and harvesting in early spring can prevent this.

Eat

Leeks are versatile vegetables. Pan-fry, stir-fry or simply eat them raw. Try the long, thin leeks of 'Bulgarian Giant' or the fine-flavoured French leek, 'Bleu de Solaise'.

Store

Leeks can be kept in the fridge for up to a week.

Garlic

Allium sativum

CLOVE
Plant soon after buying
Germination: 14 days

POT STARS
Grow in deep pots, at least
20cm (8in) wide and deep

GOOD COMPANIONS
Deters pests from lettuce
and cabbage

Garlic is simple to grow in pots or containers. You can plant garlic purchased from the supermarket but cloves bought from a garden centre are better suited to grow-your-own projects.

Garlic grows in well-drained, light soil. Plant in winter as the bulbs need a cold snap to trigger growth. Prepare soil by digging in compost to help keep soil aerated.

Split the bulb into cloves and pick the healthiest for planting – a single clove will produce a whole new bulb. Pick a sunny spot where your garlic can sit for several months. Autumn-planted garlic will be ready in early summer and spring-planted garlic from mid-summer to early autumn. Or lift between March and May, when the garlic is still immature, for a harvest of tasty 'wet garlic'.

Growing calendar

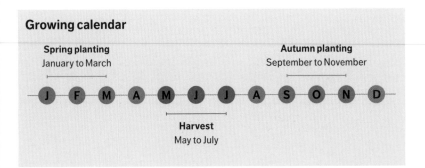

Spring planting
January to March

Autumn planting
September to November

J F M A M J J A S O N D

Harvest
May to July

SOFTNECK
Does not produce a flower stem; best for mild climates; forms smaller, tightly packed cloves; try 'Wight Cristo' for its pure white bulbs or the reliable, mild-flavoured 'Germidour'

HARDNECK
Grows a stem with an edible flower, or 'scape'; best for colder climates; forms fewer but larger cloves than softnecks; try 'Red Sicilian' for its spicy flavour or 'Lautrec Wight' for its pink cloves

Sow

Sow directly outdoors
Plant in late autumn or early spring, depending on the variety. Choose a sunny spot with well-drained soil outdoors.

Plant cloves 5cm (2in) deep with the blunt end down and the more pointed end up. Place a minimum of 10cm (4in) apart and with at least 20cm (8in) between rows. Mulch in autumn.

For autumn varieties, if the soil is soggy, plant 2.5cm (1in) deep in modules and plant out in spring. Keep in a sheltered position outdoors.

Sow in pots
To grow in containers, choose a large pot, around 20cm (8in) wide and deep. Plant around six cloves per container. Keep compost moist. Position in a sheltered spot outdoors.

Grow

Garlic is low maintenance, provided it is in a well-drained soil. If grown in the ground rather than in pots, watering isn't necessary unless the weather is very dry.

Weeds can be a problem but regular hoeing between rows, together with mulch will keep weeds at bay. Birds can be pests to young garlic plants, so protect plants with horticultural fleece.

Harvest

Yellow leaves are the signal that your garlic is ready below ground. Harvest autumn-planted garlic around June and spring-planted garlic a little later. Don't pull by the stem as it can easily snap.

Lever bulbs up gently with a hand fork before the leaves wilt to avoid rot

Elephant garlic
Allium ampeloprasum

Produces big, fat, sweet-tasting cloves that are milder in taste than traditional garlic. Does best planted in September or October, in full sun and moist conditions.

Around June, when the flower stalks are 20cm (8in) tall and the leaves are yellow, stop watering for a few days. Then loosen the soil and lift. Dry off the bulb before storing until ready to use.

Eat

'WET' GARLIC: These immature garlic bulbs can be harvested between March and May. Nutty and mild in flavour, wet garlic tastes lovely fresh or cooked. Try the chopped leaves in pesto.

ELEPHANT GARLIC: These giant bulbs can be cooked like asparagus and are also wonderful roasted. Tender scapes (the stalks that bear the garlic flower) can be fried and served with scrambled eggs.

Store

Cut away leaves, stems and roots. Place the bulbs in a dry, cool and airy place. You can also freeze them unpeeled and remove cloves as you need them.

Root
& tuberous
vegetables

Beetroot/Beet

Beta vulgaris

SEEDS
Storage: up to 4 years
Germination: 8–12 days

POT STARS
Try 'Pablo' for growing
baby beets in containers

GOOD COMPANIONS
Grow near brassicas, garlic,
carrots and parsnips

A descendant of the wild sea beets of the Mediterranean coast, this root veg is enjoying a culinary revival. Gone are the days when beetroot was only served saturated in malt vinegar.

It is now better understood just how chock-full with nutrition beetroot is, and how tasty. It is full of antioxidants and tastes wonderful baked, grated, roasted or juiced. But it is arguably at its best when eaten raw.

Beetroot is very simple to grow in the right spot. It needs an open site, and a rich but light soil with high levels of nitrogen.

Plant several crops over the growing season for a regular harvest, and pick when the root is the size of a golf ball.

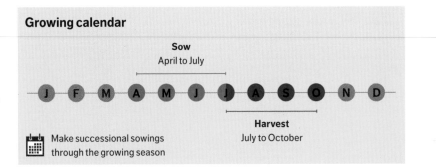

Growing calendar

Sow
April to July

J F M A M J J A S O N D

Harvest
July to October

Make successional sowings
through the growing season

RED
Try 'Boltardy' for delicious, smooth skins or 'Detroit Dark Red' for sweetness

RED AND WHITE
Grow 'Barbabietola di Chioggia' for its quirky concentric rings and mild flavour

WHITE
'Albina Vereduna' is perfect with fish or poultry and has a vitamin-rich top leaf

ORANGE-YELLOW
Sweet-tasting 'Burpee's Golden' has vibrant golden flesh and is great in salads

Sow

Sow in pots

This method is best for round rather than cylindrical cultivars. Fill a pot 20cm (8in) in diameter and 20cm (8in) deep with compost. Firm the soil, leaving a 4cm (1½in) gap between the soil surface and the top of the pot. Sow seeds thinly, then cover with soil and water them. Thin out seedlings when they're about 5cm (2in) tall, leaving 12cm (5in) gaps between them. Keep pots weed-free and well watered.

Sow directly outdoors

A few weeks prior to sowing, remove the weeds and stones from the soil and sprinkle with blood, fish and bone. Soak for 30 minutes before sowing. Make straight rows, sowing two seeds every 10cm (4in) along the row.

Grow

Water only in dry weather. Once seedlings are 5cm (2in) tall, remove the weaker plants by snipping off at soil level (and use these thinnings in salads). Weed regularly. If the root tops poke out of the soil, cover with a compost mulch.

→ **Know how – Bolting**

Keep on top of watering in hot weather. Beetroot is tolerant of dry soil but very dry conditions and lack of water results in small, woody roots.

Harvest

You can harvest beetroot at any stage, from small to fully mature roots. Depending on the variety, this will be between seven and 13 weeks after sowing. The smaller the roots, the more tender and sweet they are. Lift by the leaves and loosen from the soil with a trowel.

For a supply of beetroot through the summer, sow seeds every 2–3 weeks

Eat

When boiling, scrub the skin but don't cut it as cut beetroot loses flavour. Keep the skins on when roasting. Eat raw – sliced or grated – with a dip.

Beet greens are tasty and highly nutritious but often get thrown away. Instead, when you harvest the roots, remove the foliage, leaving a stub of stem on each root. Eat them boiled or steamed.

Store

Roots can be stored in the ground and lifted when needed – though they eventually become woody. Cover with a layer of straw or cardboard and they will last until March. But if the weather is very cold, store indoors. To store fresh young leaves for a few days, rinse and dry, and keep in a plastic bag in the fridge.

Carrots

Daucus carota subsp. *sativus*

SEEDS
Storage: up to 3 years
Germination: 16–21 days

POT STARS
Try 'Early Nantes', 'Royal Chantenay' or 'Parmex'

GOOD COMPANIONS
Plant near spring onions, mint and leeks

Carrots are edible taproots and closely related to fennel, parsnip and parsley, as well as to wild carrot.

Despite their ubiquity, carrots need a bit of attention to grow them well: they are slow to germinate and can be entirely decimated by carrot fly (see p.155).

Being root vegetables, carrots are especially sensitive to soil conditions. Stony soils create stunted or forked produce, so a deep, finely textured soil is imperative if you'd like to grow a long, slender variety. However, short varieties, which have shallow roots, can be grown in heavy, stony conditions.

Carrots are suitable for gardens large and small, and as a quick-growing crop, you can sow them regularly in small batches for a continuous supply. You can also sow seeds in containers.

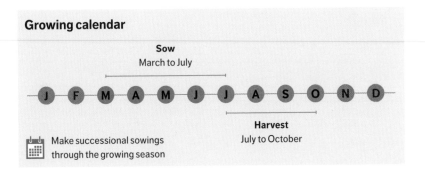

Growing calendar

Sow
March to July

J F M A M J J A S O N D

Harvest
July to October

Make successional sowings through the growing season

153

BALL-TYPE
Small roots; good choice for heavy clay soil and pots; try 'Paris Market'

CHANTENAY
A stout, sweet-tasting variety that can be grown in rocky soil

DANVERS
Stocky and deep orange. Great in juices

NANTES
Long, slender and easy to grow. Tastes sweet and crisp

Sow

Sow in pots

Fill a rectangular container at least 20cm (8in) deep with a mix of compost, soil and horticultural sand. Sprinkle seeds in drills over the top of the soil surface. Cover gently with a 1cm (½in) layer of soil.

When seedlings appear after about three weeks, remove the weakest plant of every four, so that the remaining seedlings have space to grow. Leave gaps between of 5–7.5cm (2–3in). Keep soil moist.

Sow directly outdoors

Position early carrots in a sheltered spot and maincrop carrots in an open, sunny site. Carrots are a cool-season crop, so they prefer low temperatures and natural light levels. In autumn, cultivate the soil, adding well-rotted manure in preparation for sowing spring seeds. A few weeks before the last spring frost has passed, remove weeds and rake lumps out of the seedbed. Make shallow rows 1cm (½in) deep, spaced 20cm (8in) apart.

Mix seeds with sand, and sow a thin line of the seed sand mix along the row. Cover gently, without disturbing seeds. Water using a fine rose so seeds don't wash away.

Grow

Thin to 7.5cm (3in) apart when large enough to handle. Water when soil is dry. Cover the tops of the roots with compost to prevent getting green carrot tops.

→ Know how – Banishing carrot fly

Carrot flies are attracted by the smell that carrots give off when they are thinned. The flies can ruin an entire crop. To avoid this pest, sow seeds in early summer, thin seedlings in the early evening and remove thinnings from the plot. Sowing spring onions amongst your carrots will also deter these pests: they hate the smell.

Harvest

Early varieties will be ready around nine weeks after sowing; maincrop carrots take three months.

Loosen the soil around the root with a trowel and pull straight out of the ground. Pull up carrots as soon as they are big enough to eat or leave in the ground to grow bigger – though you may sacrifice flavour.

Use carrot leaves to make pesto

Eat

Eating whole and unpeeled preserves more vitamins and minerals but peeled carrots taste sweeter. Drizzle with honey and roast them or turn them into veggie burgers.

Store

Twist off the tops but don't wash. Store in a box somewhere cool, dry and frost-free for up to four months. Or keep in the ground until you need them.

Parsnips

Pastinaca sativa

SEEDS
Storage: up to 1 year
Germination: 10–30 days

GOOD COMPANIONS
Garlic, onions, potatoes, radishes

Parsnips are fleshy, edible, cream-coloured taproots that can be cooked or eaten raw.

Once established, these veg are pretty laid back. They are content to grow in semi-shade or sun and are hardy – frosts give them a sweeter, nuttier flavour. Leave them in the ground and harvest when needed.

These root veg need work to get going, however. The soil must be deep, loose and stone-free and the seeds have to be coaxed into life. Weeds must be controlled from the outset.

Parsnips have a growing period of around 100 days, so ensure you have a space in your garden plot where they can linger a while.

Growing calendar

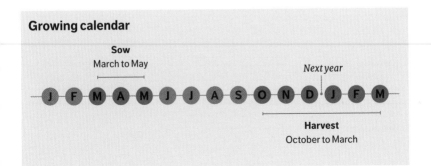

Sow
March to May

Next year

J F M A M J J A S O N D J F M

Harvest
October to March

Varieties

Parsnips are classified according to their shape – bulbous, wedge or bayonet. Bulbous are stocky types but because their roots don't grow too large, they're ideal in a limited space or in shallow, stony soils (try 'Avonresister'). Wedge types are long and broad (try 'All American'), while bayonet parsnips are long and narrow (try 'Hollow Crown'). Many cultivars, such as 'Albion' and 'Palace', are now canker-resistant (see opposite), but not all are, so check.

Sow

Germinate

Use newly bought seeds or those harvested from plants the previous summer. To give seeds a head start, you can germinate them indoors. Around 10 days before planting outside, place seeds on a wet paper towel and place in an airtight container. Keep at room temperature. Check regularly for signs of germination, and to ensure the paper towel doesn't dry out.

Sow directly outdoors

Don't rush to get your seeds outdoors. Parsnip crops often fail because they've been planted out too early, before the soil has had chance to warm up. Wait until the soil is warm enough for you to sit on it comfortably – ideally, imagine whether you'd do this without clothes on!

Plant your pre-germinated seeds in moist, deep soil where stones have been removed (to avoid crooked veg). Sow two seeds every 15cm (6in), leaving 30cm (12in) between rows.

Sow quick-growing radish seeds (see pp.160–162) between your parsnips at the same time. The radishes will be visible within days, marking your rows clearly and enabling you to hoe any weeds sprouting nearby.

→ Know how – Canker

Parsnip canker is a fungus that discolours and rots plant roots and foliage. The condition occurs in autumn and winter. The best line of defence is to grow resistant varieties. But crop rotation will also help, as will sowing as late as possible; smaller parsnips are less prone to the disease.

Grow

Remove the weakest seedling when plants have reached around 2.5cm (1in) tall. Do not use these thinnings as micro greens as the seedlings are poisonous. Keep weeded and only water in very dry periods.

Harvest

Leave in the ground until required, ideally after the first frosts. Use a fork to loosen the soil and dig around the parsnip with a trowel before attempting to lift it. As leaves die back in winter, mark rows with a cane, allowing you to find your parsnips when you need them.

Parsnips break up soil, creating fine-textured beds for peas and beans

Eat & store

Parsnips are more nutritious if you eat them with the peel on; just scrub gently or peel very thinly to remove dirt. For something a bit different, try parsnip hash browns. Uncooked parsnips keep in the fridge for a week.

Radishes

Raphanus sativus

SEEDS
Storage: up to 5 years
Germination: 4–8 days

POT STARS
Well-suited to containers.
Try 'Sparkler'

GOOD COMPANIONS
Squash, beans, peas,
lettuce, cucumber

Crisp and peppery, radishes are one of the quickest crops you can grow. They are ready to harvest in as little as four weeks. They do well in sun or part-shade and will obligingly fill gaps around other crops. You can also plant seeds every week in spring to enjoy radishes all summer long.

They can even be grown in used growbags at the end of the summer. Simply cut a panel out of the top of the growbag and sow in short rows.

Winter radishes – known as mooli daikon – are sown in late summer. They need loose, friable soil and cool temperatures. Try sowing in a potato bed after all the spuds have been lifted.

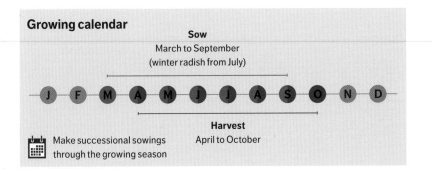

Growing calendar

Sow
March to September
(winter radish from July)

J F M A M J J A S O N D

Harvest
April to October

Make successional sowings
through the growing season

161

SUMMER
Round, oval or long; often ruby red with white tips; try 'French Breakfast', 'Mirabeau' with long roots, 'Sparkler' and 'Scarlet Globe' which are oval roots for pots

WINTER
A larger root for soups, stews and stir-fries; try mooli daikon varieties or 'Red Flesh' which looks like a miniature watermelon

SEED PODS
Grown for their edible, spicy seed pods rather than their roots; try 'Rat-tailed'

Sow

Sow in pots

Use a deep, 30cm (12in) diameter pot with drainage holes in the bottom. Fill with multi-purpose compost almost to the top, scatter seeds thinly across the surface, then cover with a little more compost. Water with a watering can fitted with a fine rose. Position in a sunny spot.

Sow directly outdoors

Rake over the soil and remove any weeds. Make trenches about 1cm (½in) deep and 25cm (10in) apart. Sow the seeds about 5cm (2in) apart along the trenches. Cover with a thin layer of fine soil and pat it down firmly. Water with a watering can fitted with a fine rose.

Grow

Don't let radishes dry out, but take care to water in dry weather to prevent roots splitting. If leaves appear tightly packed together, the seedlings could be overcrowded. Carefully pull out some of the young plants, creating more space for those that remain and aiming for a gap of 2.5cm (1in), and 15cm (6in) for winter cultivars.

⊕ Know how – Catch crops

To make the most use of your available growing area, try sowing a catch crop of radishes between rows of other vegetables, such as peas, onions, parsnips, carrots or potatoes. Or sow fast-growing radishes as markers for slow-growing veg. The radishes will grow before the other veg require the space. They help you distinguish between your rows of veg and any weeds sprouting around them.

Harvest

Radishes are ready in as few as four weeks but leave longer for varieties with larger roots. Small varieties are best eaten young; older roots can be hollow and have a woody texture. Twist and pull out of the ground as required.

Baby leaf greens are edible – use them to spice up salads

Eat

RAW: Eat raw as a crunchy snack accompanied by sea salt, bread and a decent beer. Slice the roots and add to salads or relishes. Delicious mixed with carrot, apple, raisins, mint and sesame seeds as a salad.

ROAST: Chop and mix with oil, honey and lemon juice, and cook in a medium oven for 20 minutes.

MOOLI DAIKON: Try this grated and fried or make into breadcrumb-coated mooli cakes. In Japan, mooli is often served pickled.

¼ actual size

SEED POTATOES
Use in year of purchase

POT STARS
Any large, deep container
will do. Try 'Patio Planter
Collection'

GOOD COMPANIONS
Beans, sweetcorn,
cabbage

Potatoes

Solanum tuberosum

Considered one of the most important food crops in the world, there are countless varieties of potato. First earlies and second early potatoes – commonly referred to as new potatoes – tend to be small and waxy. Maincrop potatoes are larger, given that they spend longer in the ground. All varieties are thought to benefit from 'chitting' prior to planting (see p.168).

To grow your own, you'll need seed potatoes, which are specially grown tubers for planting. Potatoes are suited to most soil types. They are a good choice for new plots because the developing tubers help to break up heavy soil.

These veg are also brilliant in large containers. You can buy ready-made potato planters or sacks, or even recycle an old dustbin or tub – just pierce drainage holes in the bottom before filling with soil.

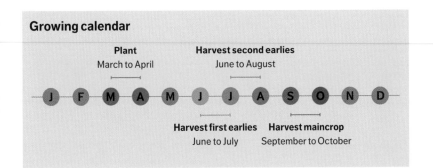

Growing calendar

| | Plant | Harvest second earlies |
| | March to April | June to August |

J F **M** **A** **M** **J** **J** **A** **S** **O** N **D**

Harvest first earlies — **Harvest maincrop**
June to July — September to October

165

Varieties

Once you've decided whether you'd like to harvest an early or maincrop potato, you can then choose a variety based on how you'd like to eat it. Varieties described as floury are best for mashing, roasting or baking. Waxy potatoes are great for boiling. But some varieties are good cooked all ways.

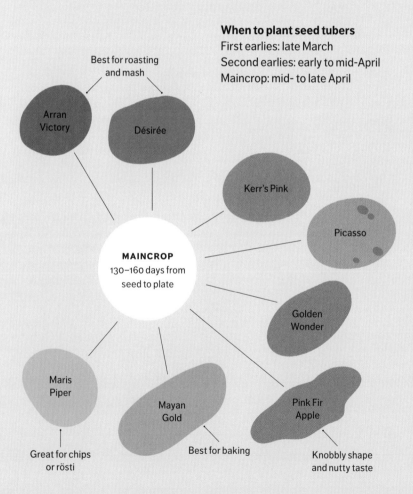

When to plant seed tubers
First earlies: late March
Second earlies: early to mid-April
Maincrop: mid- to late April

Best for roasting and mash

Arran Victory

Désirée

Kerr's Pink

Picasso

MAINCROP
130–160 days from seed to plate

Golden Wonder

Maris Piper

Mayan Gold

Pink Fir Apple

Great for chips or rösti

Best for baking

Knobbly shape and nutty taste

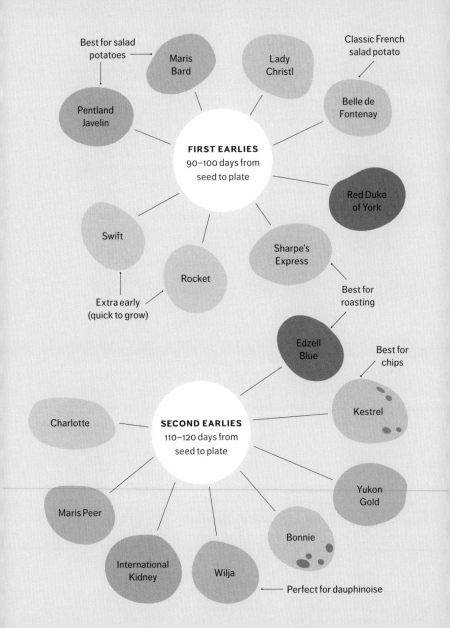

Best for salad potatoes →

Maris Bard

Lady Christl

Classic French salad potato

Belle de Fontenay

Pentland Javelin

FIRST EARLIES
90–100 days from seed to plate

Red Duke of York

Swift

Sharpe's Express

Rocket

↑ Extra early (quick to grow)

Best for roasting

Edzell Blue

Best for chips

SECOND EARLIES
110–120 days from seed to plate

Kestrel

Charlotte

Yukon Gold

Maris Peer

Bonnie

International Kidney

Wilja

— Perfect for dauphinoise

Chitting

It is essential to 'chit' your potatoes, particularly earlies. Chitting allows small shoots in the top of the potatoes to develop longer shoots before planting. Chit in late winter. Place seed potatoes in egg boxes or in a seed tray so that the top, or 'rose' end – the end with most eyes – points upwards. Keep indoors in a light, dry, frost-free place that is out of direct sunlight. Six weeks later, shoots will have grown and the seed potatoes are ready to plant out.

Grow

In a raised bed or border

Once risk of frost has passed, make a narrow trench about 15cm (6in) deep on a sunny site. Plant the tubers with their shoots pointing upwards.

Plant earlies 30cm (12in) apart with 60cm (2ft) between rows, and second early and maincrop 45cm (18in) apart with 75cm (30in) between rows. Draw soil over the rows and water in well. Add slug deterrents between the tubers.

In a sack or container

Add 10cm (4in) of compost to the bottom of the sack or container. Put the tubers on top and cover with the same amount of compost again. Water. As the stems emerge, add another layer of compost, repeating until the container is almost full.

⊙ Know how – Earthing up

When stems reach around 20cm (8in) tall, cover the bases of the shoots and leaves with soil or compost. Do this by drawing up the soil sitting between the rows. The purpose of earthing up is to provide mulch and to keep potatoes away from the light, which turns tubers green and slightly poisonous.

→ Know how – Blight

Blight is a common fungal disease, particularly in humid weather. It turns leaf edges brown and causes them to rot. Cut off all the leaves and stems as soon as you spot blight. Earthing up will provide a barrier between tubers and fungal spores. Avoiding overhead watering can also prevent trouble.

Harvest

Lift earlies and second earlies just before flowers open. For maincrop varieties, check on your tubers when the plant leaves turn yellow. Cut the foliage down with a knife to just above the soil surface. Leave the spuds in the ground for around 10 days. Lift on a dry day. Leave them on the soil surface to dry out for a few hours, and then store.

Neither plants nor tubers will tolerate frost

Eat

Potato scones, potato soup, potato and rosemary focaccia – there's so much more to this veg than mash.

Store

Keep in a cool, dark, well-ventilated place. Avoid refrigeration, which diminishes the flavour. Young or new potatoes may be frozen.

Sweet potatoes

Ipomoea batatas

Low-fat and full of potassium, fibre and more vitamin C than ordinary potatoes, sweet potatoes are also commonly known as yams. Despite the name, this veg isn't really a potato but a member of the *Convolvulaceae* family, whose plants are often climbers with long, trailing vines.

These trailing vines are traditionally grown in warm countries but hardy cultivars are now more widely available. They are often grown as ornamental plants for their heart-shaped leaves (which happen to be edible) and trumpet-shaped flowers, which come in shades of lavender, purple and white.

Sweet potatoes range from pale-coloured types, which have a floury taste, to those with deep orange flesh and an intense sweet flavour.

¹⁄₁₀ actual size

SLIPS
Sweet potatoes are grown from 'slips'

POT STARS
Grow one slip per pot in large, deep containers – at least 35cm (14in) in diameter. Try 'O' Henry'

GOOD COMPANIONS
Plant near parsnips, beetroot and potatoes

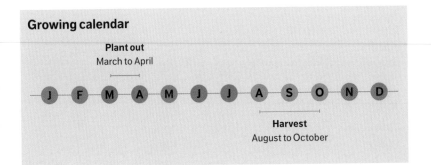

Growing calendar

Plant out
March to April

J F M A M J J A S O N D

Harvest
August to October

171

Varieties

Sweet potatoes come in many colours, both of skin and flesh, and in different shapes and sizes. But one of the key considerations when choosing is space; some vines will grow 3.5m (11½ft) or more, while bush varieties stay compact, around 1.5m (5ft). The varieties below are all vines.

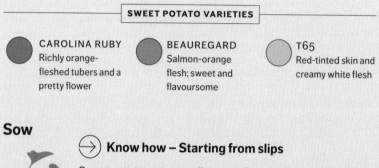

SWEET POTATO VARIETIES

CAROLINA RUBY
Richly orange-fleshed tubers and a pretty flower

BEAUREGARD
Salmon-orange flesh; sweet and flavoursome

T65
Red-tinted skin and creamy white flesh

Sow

→ Know how – Starting from slips

Sweet potatoes are usually grown from 'slips' – the long shoots of seed potatoes. Seed companies send out slips by mail during spring. When they arrive, unpack the fragile slips carefully and revive them – they look withered – in a glass of water overnight. Next day, plant the slips into deep pots of compost, burying the slip to just below its leaves. Cover with a clear plastic bag. Place on a sunny windowsill, keep the soil moist and roots will start to grow.

→ Know how – Starting your own plants

Don't grow your own slips from bought sweet potatoes. Instead, to grow them for next year, simply store a sweet potato or two from your own harvest, over-winter them and place in a pot of compost in the spring.

Plant them upright with one end pointing out of the soil. Keep the compost moist and place on a sunny windowsill. 'Eyes' will appear within weeks, followed by sprouting slips that can be cut off once they are 15cm (6in) high. Treat these just as you would bought slips.

Grow

Grow slips in a bright, frost-free position in a greenhouse or on a sunny windowsill. In early summer – May or June – when the soil has warmed up, it's time to transplant them outside or into large pots or growbags. Harden plants off before planting outdoors. They need moisture-retentive, free-draining soil and a sheltered but sunny position. It is advisable to warm the ground a few weeks prior to planting by laying black polythene over the soil. This will also suppress weeds.

Plant out, keeping plants in rows 75cm (30in) apart. Cover with cloches or fleece. If planting into a container, use the biggest one you can to give the tubers and roots room to develop, and to allow space for the plant's enthusiastic vines!

An occasional comfrey liquid feed every other week will be appreciated. Keep up the watering. Train vines onto a trellis to keep them tidy.

Harvest

It takes 4–5 months for the tubers to grow. When the leaves start to die back or if there's any sign of frost, then it's time to harvest. Loosen soil and lift out the tubers; unlike regular potatoes, sweet potato tubers are delicate and bruise easily.

Eat

Rub – don't scrub – the soil off the skins. Sweet potatoes are used as a source of alcohol and are fermented to make a Japanese spirit known as imō-jōchu.

Store

Cure freshly dug sweet potatoes for 7–10 days to improve flavour, heal bruises and cuts in the skin, and enable the sweet potatoes to be kept for longer. Place in a crate or box, ideally so they are not touching each other, and put somewhere warm.

Herbs
& edible
flowers

Herb horticulture

There are many more varieties of kitchen herbs than supermarkets would have us believe, so experiment. Plant in pots and snip leaves and sprigs as you need them.

Chives
Allium spp.
Grown for its foliage, which has a mild onion flavour. Grows in a variety of colours and flavours. The purple flowers are also edible – use as a salad garnish. Chop them into salads or onto baked potatoes. Great with cheese.

Chervil
Anthriscus cerefolium
Delicate, feathery leaves have a mild, aniseed flavour. Gather leaves before flowering, starting with outer ones. Sprinkle over creamy courgette/zucchini soup. Tastes delicious with peas.

French tarragon
Artemisia dracunculus
Slender, greyish green, aromatic leaves are perfect with fish or chicken. Position in sun and protect from rain. Grows well in containers. Use leaves to flavour vinegar. Mix with breadcrumbs for a herb crust.

Fennel
Foeniculum vulgare
Not to be confused with Florence fennel, the variety grown for its swollen bulbs. Aromatic seeds of this one can be used in cakes, bread and stuffing. Harvest young leaves. Eat sprouted seeds in salads.

Curry plant

Helichrysum italicum
Small, bushy, evergreen shrub. Excellent for attracting bees and other beneficial insects. Curry-scented leaves have a mild flavour when cooked. Try with cream cheese. Add sprigs to dishes for a slight curry flavour.

Bay

Laurus nobilis
Evergreen shrub with glossy leaves. Grow near a south or west-facing wall. Use leaves fresh or dried to flavour meat, curries, soups and stews. Essential for making spaghetti bolognaise and beef bourguignon.

Lemon balm

Melissa officinalis
Great for wildlife. Leaves have a pleasant, lemon aroma. Eat fresh young leaves with fish, meat and cheese. Bake into a cake or eat with lemon meringue ice cream.

Coriander/cilantro

Coriandrum sativum
Prefers a warm, dry, light soil. Fast-growing. Whole plant is edible but leaves harvested before flowering are best. Asian cuisine uses the seeds and leaves in curry. Add to fish tacos for fruity vibrancy.

Herb horticulture

Oregano
Origanum vulgare
Thrives in sandy soil. Loved by butterflies. Pretty, small, purple flowers. Dried leaves are more flavoursome than fresh ones. Widely used in Greek and Italian cuisine with tomato, lamb and salads.

Parsley
Petroselinum crispum
Flat-leaf parsley has a grassy flavour; curly-leaf parsley is sweeter. Pour a full kettle of warm water over seeds to kick-start germination. Harvest regularly to encourage further growth. Try in potato dumplings or chop into sauces, soups, salads and cheese.

Mint
Mentha spp.
Have fun experimenting with its many varieties. Keep in a pot, as these plants are invasive. Apple mint is delicious with lamb, tzatziki and tabbouleh. Add boiled water to a sprig of spearmint for tea. Grow basil mint for flavouring oils and vinegars, and ginger mint for fruit salads.

Rosemary
Rosmarinus officinalis
Sun-loving, fully-hardy, evergreen perennial. White rosemary is fantastic with lamb. Try 'Miss Jessopp's Upright' in tomato sauces.

⊕ Know how – Growing herbs

Most herbs can be container-grown. But they have varying levels of frost-tolerance and climatic requirements, so familiarize yourself with specific requirements before sowing seeds.

Sage
Salvia spp.
Frost-hardy perennial. Leaves come in a wide range of colours and variegated forms. Rich flavour used for stuffing and cooked meats. But varieties such as fruit-scented sage are delicious in a fruit salad.

Thyme
Thymus spp.
Grows in a range of foliage, flowers and flavours. Retains lots of flavour when dried, so perfect for storing. Eat lemon thyme in chicken and fish dishes. Try caraway-scented thyme for beef recipes.

Basil
Ocimum basilicum
Easy to grow and many varieties to try. Needs heat to germinate. Sow indoors in small pots. Snip back to just above a pair of leaves, where new shoots will grow. Fresh leaves can be torn into pesto and onto pizza. Try Thai lime basil or cinnamon basil for stir-fries and rice.

Experiment with edible flowers

Edible flowers bring quirky vibrancy to the dinner table.
For the best flavour, pick in the morning, at peak bloom,
and eat the same day.

Pot marigold
Calendula officinalis
Regular deadheading keeps it flowering. Pollinated by
bees. Use vitamin-rich leaves to brighten up salads.
Dried petals can be used in soups and cakes.

Pinks, carnation, Sweet William
Dianthus spp.
Grow fragrant varieties for cakes. Sweet William petals
can be used in ice cream, sorbet and fruit salad. Use pink
petals in salads. Make great cut flowers to bring indoors.

Sunflower
Helianthus annuus
Sow direct into the ground or start in pots. Buds, seeds
and petals can be eaten. Seed kernels can be eaten raw
or roasted. Cook buds like globe artichokes. Add the
leaves to salads.

Scented pelargonium
Pelargonium spp.
Small white, purple or pink flowers. Rose, nutmeg or
lemon-flavoured flowers can be used in sorbets and ice
cream. The leaves can be added to blackberry and
apple pies.

Make sure you know what flower you are picking and that it is safe to eat before consuming it. Only eat flowers that have been grown without pesticides. When removing petals, cut off any white or non-coloured areas at the base of the petal – they can taste bitter. Consult an edible flower cookbook to determine how individual species should be prepared and eaten.

Nasturtium
Tropaeolum majus
Needs sun and moist soil. Pickle immature green pods to make 'capers'. Fresh leaves and flowers have a hot, watercress flavour. Stuff flowers with cream cheese. Make nasturtium butter by mixing flowers and leaves with butter.

Rose
Rosa spp.
Grows in any well-drained soil. Petals are delicate and sweet. Crystallize fragrant petals for cake decoration. Turn rose hips into jelly and syrups or dry and infuse for a tea.

Begonia
Begonia x *tuberhybrida*
Will flower up to the first frosts. Petals have a light citrus flavour and are great in sandwiches. Dip flowers whole into yoghurt for an unusual treat. Avoid eating if you suffer from gout, kidney stones and rheumatism.

Daylily
Hemerocallis spp.
Easy to grow, but avoid planting in heavy shade. Flowers can be eaten raw when fully open. Roots are edible raw or cooked. Eat in salads and stir-fries. Only daylilies (*Hemerocallis*) can be eaten. Other types of lily are poisonous.

Weeds you can eat

Weeds can wreak havoc in your garden but there is a joyful side to them.

Dandelion
Taraxacum officinale
A food plant for hoverflies and other beneficial insects. Its leaves are full of antioxidants and vitamins. Throw blanched leaves into salads, pies and soups, or sauté them. Flowers can be turned into dandelion wine.

Stinging nettle
Urtica dioica
Hugely beneficial to wildlife, particularly butterflies. Wear gloves when harvesting young leaves in spring. Cooking destroys its sting. Used in Cornish Yarg cheese. Try in pesto and risotto. Make into cleansing soups, cordials and beer.

Chickweed
Stellaria media
A prolific self-seeder, chickweed is available all year. Grows almost anywhere. Highly nutritious. Eat tender leaves raw in salad. Turn into pakoras or pesto. The ground-up seeds will thicken breads and soups. Generally considered safe but do not eat in large quantities.

As with any wild food, make sure you are certain what plants you're picking, and that they are safe to eat.

Jack-by-the-hedge (garlic mustard)

Alliaria petiolata

Found near hedges and edge of woodland. Small, white flowers attract pollinators. Leaves have a mild mustard and garlic flavour. Wilt leaves and add to a potato salad. Chop into sandwiches, frittatas and vinaigrettes. Generally considered safe but do not eat in large quantities.

Ground elder

Aegopodium podagraria

A rampant weed of hedgerows and gardens. Pick the leaves when young; they have a parsley-like flavour. Blanch them, fry with onions and turn into a quiche. Or make into croquettes.

Watercress

Nasturtium officinale

Grows alongside flowing water. Harvest all year round. Highly wholesome weed, high in iron. If harvested from the wild, cook the leaves first. Their pungent, spicy flavour tastes great with mackerel and horseradish.

Cultivate a cocktail garden

Why not toast your efforts in the garden with a cocktail made from your own produce?

Mint
Mentha spp.
All mint is easy to grow and look after. Moroccan spearmint is sweeter and less pungent than peppermint. Mint is an essential ingredient of a mojito or a julep.

Strawberries
Fragaria x *ananassa*
Give this fruit sun, shelter and a fertile soil. Grow summer-fruiting strawberries for daiquiris. Alpine strawberries taste fab with ice cream.

Cucamelons
Melothria scabra
Exotic but easy to grow in a mild climate (see pp.106–107). These mini watermelons add a lime-and-cucumber flavour. Try with gin and tonic, and martini.

Borage
Borago officinalis
A bee magnet that's easy to grow from seed. Freeze its star-shaped, blue flowers in ice cubes. A classic garnish for Pimm's or make into strawberry-borage cocktails.

Lavender and rosemary
Lavandula angustifolia, *Rosmarinus officinalis*
Infuse both these herbs in gin. Lavender makes a gorgeous garnish in a champagne flute. Try rosemary with sloe gin.

⊖ Know how – Muddling herbs

Don't crush, shred or tear leaves as that will make your cocktail taste bitter. Instead, for cocktails with an intense fresh-herb flavour, 'muddle' or mash your leaves. You needn't buy a special muddler tool; the end of a rolling pin will do. Put your herb in the bottom of a thick glass, along with the other ingredients in your recipe. Press lightly and twist gently a few times.

Basil
Ocimum basilicum
Offer basil a sunny, sheltered spot and lots of food. Combine with lemon and mix into a margarita or try in tequila. Create a cocktail with raspberry, basil and liquorice root.

Lemon verbena
Aloysia citrodora
Position it against a sunny wall and come autumn, protect from frost. Makes a brilliant, aromatic container plant. Imparts a sweet citrus flavour to sangrias or vodka lemonades.

Coriander/cilantro
Coriandrum sativum
Pick young leaves for using fresh. Add them to tomato-based tipples. Mix with gin, cucumber, lime, ginger ale and ice.

Dill
Anethum graveolens
Water plants well, especially in a hot spell. Combine with grapefruit soda, blanco tequila and cucumber.

Problem solving

As you watch your garden grow, it is likely that you will encounter one challenge or another – be it troublesome weeds, peckish animals, or woeful plants for no discernible reason. Here are our tips on how to nip some of these troubles in the bud.

Wrangling with weeds

Weeds compete with your plants for light, nutrients and moisture. They can take over beds and quickly get established from seed or tiny fragments of root. While they need to be managed on the veg plot, weeds also support many types of wildlife. So keep them under control when it comes to your crops, but otherwise leave them alone.

It's useful to understand the life cycle of weeds as that determines how to tackle them. Weeds, like all plants, have four stages of growth (seedling, stem, root and leaf growth, seed production, and maturity) and will either complete their life cycle in one year, two years, or three years or more. But remember, whatever the weed, you need to take action to eradicate it before it produces seed.

⊖ Know how – Avoiding herbicides

Though a nuisance to gardeners, weeds do have their uses, providing food for birds, bees and other beneficial insects.

Organic growers manage weeds without herbicides, using a combination of physical deterrents and cultural practices instead. Crop rotation is perhaps the most effective preventative measure. Growing different crops in succession means that no one weed is given the chance to dominate.

As well as hoeing and hand-forking pesky plants away, environmentally aware methods also include regular use of green manure and mulching.

Laying down weed-suppressant sheeting or thick cardboard over beds for a growing season, or no-dig cultivation are other methods available to you. Flame guns are eco-friendly tools that can be used to scorch weeds.

Annual weeds

Annual weeds reproduce by seed, so hoe them out before this stage. Summer annual weeds germinate in spring and produce seed in summer. Winter annuals germinate in the autumn and flower and set seed in late spring or early summer.

Groundsel
Senecio vulgaris
Flowers and sets seed through the year. Smothers young crops and causes black root rot in peas. Hoe out of the soil surface at regular, 14-day intervals.

Chickweed
Stellaria media
Grows in cool, humid conditions. Seeds germinate at any time of year and survive the hardest frost. Complete burial is the most effective treatment. Chaffinches will eat the seeds, as will several species of ground beetle.

Shepherd's purse
Capsella bursa-pastoris
Grows in sun or shade. Typically seen from May to October, each plant produces around 4,000 seeds. Prevent flowering and seeding by cultivating soil with a hoe.

Hairy bittercress
Cardamine hirsuta
Grows on bare ground, walls and the surface of containers. It can disperse new seeds far away from the parent. Fork out at first sight.

Other annual weeds: fat hen (*Chenopodium album*), black bindweed (*Fallopia convolvulus*) and annual meadow grass (*Poa annua*).

Perennial weeds

These weeds reproduce vegetatively by creeping stems, rhizome roots and tubers, as well as by seed. It's tricky to control them. No-dig cultivation is effective for clearing large areas or try suppressing them with sheets of thick black plastic. Never throw perennial weeds into a compost bin!

Couch grass
Elymus repens
This weed forms a dense mat that excludes other vegetation. It flowers from May to September and spreads by rhizomes as quick as a flash. Once it's in your soil, cultivate the ground regularly by hoeing and exposing rhizomes to dry air. Grow cover crops to shade seedlings: when shaded, they die.

Curled dock
Rumex crispus
You'll find it in gardens from spring to autumn. Seeds are produced from tiny brown flowers, which appear in abundance come summertime. It can re-grow after being hoed away. Weed deeply to remove the taproot before the plant sets seed. Shading with cover crops may also work over winter, as new plants require light.

Japanese knotweed
Fallopia japonica
This persistent weed will rapidly colonize and suppress any plant in its way with tall thickets and a dense leaf canopy. It can grow up to 10cm (4in) a day and can regenerate from a small piece of root. Pulling or digging out the weed has some effect if repeated every few weeks, but you must burn all waste plant material. If you find this weed, seek advice.

Hedge bindweed

Calystegia sepium

Long stems scramble and choke plants. It flowers from June to October and sets seed from September to October. Fork out, remove and burn all traces of rootstock and rhizomes in autumn and winter. In spring, dig out new shoots.

Other perennial weeds: ground elder (*Aegopodium podagraria*), horsetail (*Equisetum arvense*), blackberry bramble (*Rubus fruticosus*) and creeping buttercup (*Ranunculus repens*).

Biennial weeds

These weeds complete their growth in two years. The first, the plant produces leaves and the second, it produces fruits and seeds. They are most effectively dealt with in the seedling stage.

Caper spurge

Euphorbia lathyris

Found in fields and gardens, its seeds are poisonous and its milky sap can irritate the skin. The flowers are inconspicuous and yellow-green. The seeds, which remain viable for long periods, disperse widely (with the help of ants). Lift with a hoe or hand fork before the plant sets seed.

⊙ Know how – Stale seedbeds

Stale seedbeds involve leaving the ground bare for a few weeks before you plant out your crop seeds, which coaxes weed seeds lurking just below the surface to germinate. Start by cultivating the soil as you would for your crops. With a rake, work over the bed, breaking the soil down into a fine 'tilth' – it should look like the top of an apple crumble. The weed seeds should then reveal themselves and you can kill them off with a hoe!

Plant-nibbling creatures

Creatures big and small inevitably cause unwanted damage to crops. Aiming to eliminate all 'pests' using chemical controls can be harmful to the environment, so consider other forms of intervention. Birds, bugs and amphibians – natural predators of slugs and aphids – are the gardener's greatest allies.

Snails

These common garden critters chew holes in leaves, stems, flowers and bulbs. Go on a torchlit search at the end of a wet weather day to hand-pick snails into a container. They can be moved elsewhere in the garden or put in a compost heap.

Where possible, encourage hedgehogs and toads by providing moist hiding spots. Hedgehogs will be drawn to piles of fallen leaves, dead vegetation and twigs. Snails are also a tasty meal for song thrushes and spotted flycatchers.

Slugs

Feeding at night, slugs inflict most damage during warm, humid spells, making holes in foliage and leaving slimy trails in their wake.

You could refrain from planting seedlings outside until they are sturdy young plants. Give these 'teen' plants some protection from slugs with cloches. Raking over your soil in winter will expose slug eggs for birds to eat.

Similar to snails, hand-picking slugs on a mild evening reduces the damage to your crops. Hedgehogs, slow worms, frogs and toads also help keep own top of them.

Pigeons

Pigeons peck away at foliage until all that remains is a skeleton of stalks and leaf veins. Anti-bird netting prevents access to crops. For a low-budget solution, drape a net over bamboo canes, fence posts or stakes, and anchor it to the ground with bent wire.

Cats

Cats like to use vegetable gardens as toilet areas. Nice! You'll spot strong-smelling excrement in the beds or buried in holes. Try netting and keeping soil watered (which cats don't like). You can also cover bare areas with planted lollipop sticks, which deter cats from roaming.

Ants

Ants won't do your garden too much harm. The main problem is they have fostered some ecological pact with aphids – which are an issue. Ants protect the aphids from predators and carry them to host plants. In return, the ants get first dibs of the honeydew that the aphids excrete.

Ant colonies are best left: a new colony will quickly claim the territory of a destroyed nest. So why not make a home for insect-eating birds instead, attracting them with watering spots, perches or bird boxes?

Rabbits

Rabbits feed between dusk and dawn but can also help themselves during the day. You'll notice stems razed clean to the ground, and holes and scrapes in lawns and beds. Rabbit-proof fencing is a costly option so instead protect individual plants with wire-netting barriers.

Tiny bugs

Aphids
Most plants are susceptible. Aphid infestations can be seen on shoot tips, around buds and under young leaves. You can squash the infestations with your fingers (eggs are laid on lower leaves).

Blue tits, ladybirds, lacewings and hoverfly larvae, will feast on around 50 aphids a day. So grow a 'welcome mat' of plants to seduce these predators. Coriander, dill, fennel and dandelion are among the many species that will offer them shelter and other sources of food.

Cabbage whitefly
These white-winged insects love kale, cabbage, broccoli and Brussels sprouts. Small populations only infest the outer leaves of brassica plants, causing little real damage, but larger ones cause sooty black moulds to grow on the honeydew the insects leave behind.

Blast the whitefly away with a jet of water and grow marigolds and caraway to encourage natural predators, such as ladybirds and lacewings. If the infestation is serious, burn the foliage or bury it to destroy any eggs.

Glasshouse whitefly
Cucumbers, melons, tomatoes and peppers in greenhouses are vulnerable to the glasshouse whitefly, which thrives in warm conditions. Identifiable by sticky honeydew, black, sooty mould and lacklustre plants, these pests are rapid breeders. You may also see scale-like nymphs.

Inspect plants daily and act on an infestation as soon as you spot one, by removing infested leaves. Hang yellow sticky traps to catch adults.

Vine weevil

These beetles love container-grown plants, eating leaves and severing roots. They're not fussy; indoor and outdoor plants are equally vulnerable. Plants wilt and die, and their roots wither away.

Birds, frogs, toads, shrews, hedgehogs and predatory ground beetles will prey on adults and grubs. You should also inspect plant pots, flushing these nasties out by shaking pots over an upturned umbrella. You can also spread pots, benches and canes with a sticky insect barrier glue.

Two-spotted spider mite (or glasshouse red spider mite)

A prolific mite that sucks sap from cells, causing a mottled appearance and leaf loss. As it thrives in warm, dry conditions, you'll see it between March and October.

Aubergine/eggplant, cucumber, pepper and peach are at risk, with infected plants displaying yellow flecks and stunted growth. If the infestation is severe, you may even see fine, silk webs. It can be tricky to deal with as it reproduces quickly.

You can remove eggs by hand. Wash down empty greenhouses in spring to reduce the chances of a mite infestation.

Feeding plants

Feeding is a simple way for gardeners to encourage strong, healthy plants. Here are some tips to help you decide on the best option for your garden.

Fast or slow fertilizer

SOLUBLE
Readily soluble in water, serves up nutrients to roots and foliage in a jiffy

SLOW-RELEASE
Degrades slowly under the influence of organisms in the soil

CONTROL-RELEASE
Inorganic granules that release food as the soil is watered. One application keeps plants fed for months

Plants require 15 elements. Three of them – carbon, hydrogen and oxygen – come from the atmosphere. The rest come from the soil in the form of nutrients. These elements make plant cells, build leaves and help plants to flower. Major nutrients are nitrogen, phosphorus, potassium, calcium, magnesium and sulphur. Micronutrients, which are needed in smaller quantities, are iron, manganese, copper, zinc, boron and molybdenum. Adding fertilizers doesn't improve soil health, so make sure you still mulch and cultivate your soil.

Fertilizer replenishes stores that have been washed away from the soil or used up. You might dig in a 'base dressing' at planting time to encourage root growth. Or you might apply a liquid feed from a watering can to a container-grown plant during the growing season.

Add nitrogen (N) for green growth, phosphorus (P) to help plants with photosynthesis and potassium (K) to help them ripen fruit.

How to apply fertilizer

WATERING ON
Mixing soluble fertilizer in water and applying it to the base of plants

FOLIAR FEED
Spraying plant food diluted in water directly onto the leaves. Used for a quick uptake of nutrients, to correct specific deficiencies

GRANULES, POWDERS OR PELLETS
Generally added to the topsoil prior to planting

When to apply fertilizer

Broadly, feeding is done when plants are growing and when your plants are looking under par. Container plants are likely to require feeding regularly. Borders are less needy but you could add a slow-release feed to the soil in spring to give vegetable crops a boost. Vegetable crops vary in their needs, so seek out specific advice before planting.

Organic feeds

Comfrey tea: Harvested leaves are chopped up and steeped in a water-tight container for a few weeks. Contains essential plant nutrients

Seaweed: Fresh seaweed is rich in phosphorus, nitrogen and crucial trace elements

Worm tea: Worm casts are brewed with water and molasses. Rich in nutrients, vitamins and other beneficial soil organisms

Coffee grounds: Used grounds are mixed into the soil or scattered on the surface – try on blueberries and tomatoes

Vegetable woes

Sometimes plants get sick. It happens and in many cases it's quite hard to prevent. Healthy soil and disease-resistant plant varieties will stand you in good stead. But if disaster strikes, do what you can to clear away the infection and try not to get too disheartened – there's always next year.

Potato leaf roll virus

The potato plant's upper leaves will roll and have a red-orange tinge. The peach potato aphid brings the virus to the plant. Tackle the aphids to reduce the chance of spreading the virus. You should also use certified virus-free tubers or potato varieties with a high degree of resistance, such as 'Sante' or 'Saxon'.

Cucumber mosaic virus

This affects cucumber, spinach, lettuce, celery and flowers. Leaves will be distorted, have yellow patches and mottling, and curl downwards. Flowers have white streaks. Once infected, your plant is doomed; burn it and hope for better luck next time. Keep the garden free of chickweed and groundsel, as these harbour the virus.

Broad bean/fava bean rust

Broad bean leaves and stems show small, dusty, dark brown spots surrounded by a pale yellow halo. To avoid problems, space plants properly to ensure good air flow and steer clear of damp, humid soils.

If you see a small number of pustules, pick off the leaves but if many leaves are infected, destroy the plants (don't compost them), so spores can't infect the following season's crops.

Potato and tomato blight

Plants are likely to be caught in early summer and will collapse and decay. Potatoes will show a watery rot on the leaves and will then shrivel. The stem may also have lesions. Tomatoes have similar symptoms and green fruit may be disfigured by brown patches.

This blight makes its way to gardens by wind and rain. When you see signs of infection, cut potato plants down to the ground and burn them. Dig up tubers a few weeks later and burn any with signs of the disease – a red-brown decay.

Growing resistant varieties is the sensible line of defence. Try potato 'Sarpo' or 'Sarpo Axona'. Or grow first earlies, which will be ready before blight hits. Earth up potatoes (see p.168). And always water at the base of plants; don't spray.

Tomatoes grown indoors are pretty risk-free.

Club root

A fungal infection of Brussels sprouts, cauliflower, turnip and swede, this attacks from mid-summer to late autumn. Foliage turns purple and wilts in hot weather, and the root system becomes swollen.

Improving drainage and buying plants from a club root-free source will avoid problems. And if your soil is too acid – acid soil stops plants accessing the nutrients they need – you might apply 'garden lime' to raise your soil's pH well ahead of sowing. Garden lime is available in several forms but ground limestone is available at garden centres and is easy to use.

Also grow resistant varieties.

Leek rust

You'll spy orange streaks on foliage, with raised pustules. Severely affected leaves wither and die. This common fungus loves warm, humid conditions, so look out for it between mid-summer and autumn. Leeks will still be edible; just cut away the infected areas. Handle infected material as you would for broad bean rust. Too much nitrogen fertilizer leads to lots of leafy growth, which can encourage the problem. To balance the soil, use a potassium-rich feed. Crop rotation and planting resistant varieties will also help.

Blossom end rot

Black blotches will appear on your tomatoes or peppers, brought on by calcium deficiency in the soil. This problem is caused by inconsistent watering or over-feeding. Sick fruits can't be salvaged but save others by ensuring soil isn't allowed to dry out. Add mulch to the soil surface to help preserve moisture.

Bolting

Beetroot, spinach, lettuce, radish, fennel, cabbage and pak choi can flower and go to seed prematurely – known as 'bolting' or 'going to seed'. This happens when the day length changes or when there's a cold spell. You'll notice plants flowering prematurely. Bolting stops the plant putting energy into growing and makes leaves tough or bitter. Make sure the soil is moist and well fed. To be safe, buy bolt-resistant varieties.

Are your plants missing something?

If your crops are missing vital nutrients, their leaves have a way of telling you what's going on inside the plant.

NEW GROWTH

Iron: Young leaves are pale between the veins, as iron helps the formation of chlorophyll. Remedy by lowering the soil pH.

Calcium: New leaf growth is slow, and leaf tips may stick together. Occurs in very dry soil, or when watering is erratic.

OLD GROWTH

Nitrogen: Older leaves turn yellow, and the plant becomes spindly and weak. Mulch will help long term. For a quick fix, apply a nitrogen fertilizer.

Potassium: Outer leaf edge becomes scorched and ragged. Apply a potassium feed. Organic remedies include kelp meal.

Manganese: Leaves turn yellow and brown. A rare deficiency caused by alkaline soil. Apply chelated manganese.

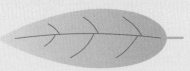

Phosphorus: Leaves develop a purple tinge. Try bone meal, or a foliar spray of sea kelp.

Magnesium: Older leaves turn yellow between veins. Leaves curve upward. Apply Epsom salts as a foliar feed and increase the soil pH with 'garden lime'.

Changing seasons

Early Spring	**Early Summer**	**Early Autumn**	**Early Winter**
March	June	September	December
Mid Spring	**Mid Summer**	**Mid Autumn**	**Mid Winter**
April	July	October	January
Late Spring	**Late Summer**	**Late Autumn**	**Late Winter**
May	August	November	February

Early Spring	**Early Summer**	**Early Autumn**	**Early Winter**
September	December	March	June
Mid Spring	**Mid Summer**	**Mid Autumn**	**Mid Winter**
October	January	April	July
Late Spring	**Late Summer**	**Late Autumn**	**Late Winter**
November	February	May	August

**Southern
Hemisphere**

Glossary

Acid A pH of less than 7

Aerate To loosen soil to allow oxygen in

Alkaline A pH of more than 7

Annual A plant that completes its life cycle in one year

Biennial A plant that completes its life cycle in two years

Chlorophyll A green plant pigment that absorbs light and enables photosynthesis

Cloche A protective structure, typically made of plastic or glass, used to cover seedlings outdoors, or warm the soil

Companion planting Growing plants close together so that one or both has a beneficial impact

Compost Growing medium. Also describes the organic material made by home composting

Crop rotation A cyclical planting system whereby crops are rotated to a new bed every year

Cultivar A plant variety that has been produced by selective breeding

Dibber A tool used for making precise planting holes

Drill A straight row in the soil in which seeds are sown

Earthing up The practice of drawing soil around a stem to aid growth

Fertile Plants that can produce viable seed, or soil that is capable of producing healthy crops

Friable A soil with a crumbly texture – ideal for planting seeds

Frost pocket An area where frost gathers, and which is subject to prolonged frosts

Frost tender A plant that cannot survive frost

Germination When a seed changes from a dormant state to active growth

Green manure A crop that is grown to be cut down into soil to improve fertility

Hardening off Introducing plants gradually from indoors to outdoors to acclimatize them

Hardy A plant that can withstand frost without protection

Lime Can be added to raise the pH of a soil. In soil, the amount of lime – or compounds of calcium – in a soil determines how acid or alkaline it is

Medium A growing mixture in which plants can be grown

Mulch Organic or inorganic matter applied to the soil surface to conserve moisture or suppress weeds, or dug into the soil to improve a soil's condition

Organic Material derived from decomposed living matter. Also a method of raising crops that uses physical, cultural and biological practices rather than fertilizers, pesticides or other chemicals

Peat Partially decayed, humus-rich vegetation formed on the surface on waterlogged soil

Perennial A plant that lives for three seasons or more

pH A measure of acidity or alkalinity in a soil

Photosynthesis The production of compounds needed for plant growth using light, water and carbon dioxide and chlorophyll

Pinching out The removal of a growing tip to encourage it to form sideshoots or flower buds

Potting on Transferring a seedling or plant to a larger pot

Pricking out Transferring seedlings from trays, seedbeds or modules to a pot or growing bed

Rhizome A creeping underground stem

Species A plant classification that describes very closely related plants that are capable of interbreeding

Tendril A modified leaf, branch or stem that enables a plant to attach itself to supports

Thinning The practice of removing seedlings to improve the quality of the remaining crop

Tuber A swollen underground organ that is used by a plant for food storage

Variety Generally used to describe any version of a plant but botanically, it is where a group of plants differs from others of the same species in a minor way

Index

To Ruth and Moira

SowHow aims to simplify gardening and encourage more people to grow their own fresh, tasty vegetables.

My thanks to everyone at Pavilion, in particular Katie Cowan and Krissy Mallett for first suggesting this book and their enthusiasm from start to finish. Thanks also to Hilary Mandleberg for her editing know-how and to Laura Russell and Claire Clewley for helping design the book. A special thank-you to Lucy Anna Scott for her brilliant writing and for being fantastic to work with.

Finally, my love and thanks to Ruth, Moira and to my parents Peter and Brenda Matson.

Pavilion
An imprint of HarperCollins*Publishers* Ltd
1 London Bridge Street
London SE1 9GF

www.harpercollins.co.uk

HarperCollins*Publishers*
Macken House,
39/40 Mayor Street Upper,
Dublin 1
D01 C9W8
Ireland

10 9 8 7 6 5 4 3 2 1

First published in Great Britain by Pavilion in 2017
An imprint of HarperCollins*Publishers* 2022

Copyright © Pavilion 2017
Text © Paul Matson 2017
Illustration © Lucy Anna Scott 2017

Paul Matson asserts the moral right to be identified as the author of this work. A catalogue record of this book is available from the British Library.

ISBN 978-1-911670-33-9

MIX
Paper | Supporting
responsible forestry
FSC™ C007454
www.fsc.org

This book is produced from independently certified FSC™ paper to ensure responsible forest management.

For more information visit: www.harpercollins.co.uk/green

Publisher's Note

You are responsible for your own safety. Correct identification of plants is extremely important. Erroneous consumption of plants can cause severe or allergic reactions. If in any doubt, do not eat.

Printed and bound by RRD in China